Com*PET*ability

Solving Behavior Problems
In Your
Multi-Cat Household

D1316428

AMY SHOJAI

Copyright

Second Print Edition, February 2017
Furry Muse Publishing
ISBN-13: 978-1944423230
ISBN-10: 1944423230

First Published by Cool Gus Publishing
First Printing, March 2013
COPYRIGHT © Amy Shojai, 2012

FURRY MUSE
PUBLISHING
P.O. Box 1904
Sherman TX 75091
(903)814-4319
amy@shojai.com

AUTHOR NOTE

Contents

PART ONE: UNDERSTANDING COM*PET*ABILITY

PART TWO: COMMON PROBLEMS AND PRACTICAL SOLUTIONS

PART THREE: COMMON MULTIPET FRUSTRATIONS

APPENDICES

PART ONE

UNDERSTANDING COM *PET*ABILITY

Chapter 1

THE JOYS OF MULTIPLE CATS

People love cats, and pets love us back. This treasured relationship has developed over many thousands of years, and continues to evolve today. Felines reflect the best parts of human nature: honesty, confidence, loving personalities, with an unbridled passion for life.

According to the American Pet Products Association 2015-2016 National Pet Owners Survey, there are 85.9 million owned cats in the United States. A previous APPA survey found:

- Thirty-three percent of U.S. households own at least one cat
- Fifty-two percent of owners own more than one cat
- On average, owners have two cats (2.2)
- More female cats are owned (80 percent) than male cats (65 percent)
- Twenty-one percent of owned cats were adopted from an animal shelter

For many of us, pets are furry family members, surrogate children, purring confidants, and a nonjudgmental support system that buoys our spirits. What a gift that they also return our love!

If a single cat provides these benefits, two or more multiplies the pleasure. Sharing your home with more than one fur-kid offers the best of all possible worlds, allowing you and your family to experience the myriad personalities cats represent. Having more than a single cat means more work, but the benefits are worth it.

Young pets clown and play, prompting our forgiving laughter even when they make mistakes. Who could resist the kitten snoozing amidst the unrolled flourish of toilet paper? Adult cats know when we've had a hard day at work, and silently commiserate with a welcome lap snuggle, lick a way tears, or transform frustration to fun with a spontaneous game of ankle tag. Pets represent milestones in human lives, because they stood by your side through the good, the bad, and the challenging, a constant reminder of love and support. When you have a couple of cats you increase the potential to have a purrfect pet partnership for every situation.

Cats come in an amazing array of looks and personalities so you can always find the right match when adding a new kid to your family. Many pets develop strong, loving relationships with each other. A confident pet can help bring a shy one out of her shell, while high energy youngsters give stuck-in-the-mud older animals a fun kick in the tail.

Sharing your home with a clowder of cats means all the humans in the house have a good chance of finding their 'heart cat' able to share not only love, but even special interests. For instance, artistic owners relish the introspection and inspiration of a furry muse. A variety of people-pet activities are available such as feline agility that increases the pleasure for both you and your pets. Refer to the Appendix for a list of some of these resources.

THE PET GENERATION

There are several reasons for the current surge in multiple pet families. You may be "adopted" by a stray mother cat with a litter on the way, and end up keeping some or all of the offspring. But most likely, the makeup of your human family evolves, prompting change in the pet count.

Blended families combine pets from both households when couples re-marry—his cats and her kittens. A newly divorced adult child may return home and bring her feline friend to join your existing pet family. Situations in which a single adult family member or friend becomes ill or dies may leave you to care for the pets. More and more, owners unexpectedly find themselves unprepared to face these situations, since they never anticipated having to deal with interspecies or multiple pet relationships.

Today, equal-opportunity pet lovers don't want to settle for one or the other—they enjoy the unique qualities of cats and dogs and share their homes with both. Dogs encourage social contact and interaction. Walking a dog guarantees meeting the neighbors and other dog lovers, and you get exercise along the way. Interacting with dogs is a pleasant and painless way to increase human exercise and promote our own health. You can find out more specifics on integrating dogs and cats, or dog-to-dog issues, in the books ComPETability: Solving Behavior Problems In Your CAT-DOG Household, and ComPETability: Solving Behavior Problems In Your Multi-DOG Household.

Cats seem to fulfill a more spiritual need, and appeal to our introspective side. Because they do not require outdoor exercise or bathroom breaks, cats may be more convenient for less active people or those who must spend long periods of time away from home. Felines may not be able to jog with an owner, but they promote emotional health benefits as well as dogs do.

Modern pet owners recognize that cats have social and emotional needs, and try to satisfy them. People facing career demands that keep them apart from their pet for long work hours may try to balance the animal's increased alone time by matchmaking him with a furry companion. In one American Animal Hospital Association survey, 44 percent of pet owners acquired a pet simply to keep another pet company.

NOBODY'S PERFECT

More pets double the fun, but also increase the potential for problems, today more than ever before. Historically, owners living in rural communities enjoyed feline companionship with few conflicts, since cats spent a large percentage of their time in the back yard, the barn or the field. That dynamic changed when pets moved into the family room, and were asked to co-exist.

It would be ideal if all our cats loved each other at first sight, played nicely together, and read our minds so they never made behavior mistakes. The truth is all owners of multiple pets will be faced with minor-to-major behavior problems. If you're experiencing problems, you are not alone!

When we welcome a cat into our lives and homes, we must accept that they are individuals with very different needs and desires. Just as human siblings don't always agree, a few squabbles are inevitable. But that does not mean owners or pets must accept rude behavior, irritating or dangerous antics, or constant warfare.

The right pet matchmaking choices must be considered to keep the fur from flying. While we love having more than one pet, the potential for conflict increases when multiple animals share the same house or apartment, the same rooms—sometimes the same bed—as human family members. Conflict upsets the pets' physical and emotional health, creates stressful or dangerous behavior problems, and damages the loving bond with owners.

WHAT'S IN THE BOOK

You're reading this book because you already know how much fun multiples can be, but you anticipate or are already challenged with behavior issues inherent to loving more than one pet. "ComPETability" provides expert behavior and care information for cohabiting cats and offers the tools needed to make educated matchmaking pet choices, prevent potential problems, and offer solutions when troubles occur.

You won't find the answer to every behavior question here, though. While much of the information in this book translates to single pet homes, and you'll sometimes be asked to train pets one at a time, the focus is on behavior problems and solutions of multiples. I've included the most common behavior challenges that directly impact the other cats living in the house.

For example, you won't find direct advice about WHAT to feed your cats, but instead I've provided tips on HOW to manage dinnertime so all the cats munch from the correct bowl and don't interfere with each other's nutrition. Rather than a section on housetraining your new kitten, discover practical tips for fixing bathroom problems that are prompted by the presence of other cats.

The majority of the book deals exclusively with how cats interact and impact each other, and ways to manage this to fix or prevent behavior problems. Expanded information is included in aggression and introduction sections, though, since these dangerous behaviors not only affect the other animals but also the owners who must manage the problem. The stress of living in a multiple cat home can increase aggression toward humans in the house or even strangers who visit. Helping your cats accept human family members, children, babies and friends is a vital part of a happy blended pet family.

The book offers three sections of information. **Part One, "Understanding Competability"** consists of three overview chapters. The one you're reading outlines the general scope of the book and introduces you to the joys of a multiple cat home. The next chapters cover cat-specific details, and a chapter offering background on behavior modification and training techniques. These opening chapters also discuss how cats learn, feline communication and social structure.

Part Two, "Common Problems and Practical Solutions" addresses the specifics of aggression, bathroom challenges, emotional issues, feeding concerns, and introductions in multi-cat households. Each of these chapters discusses the most common behavior problems you'll face with each situation, and include practical solutions. Suggestions from a variety of expert sources offer choices so you can decide which tips work best for your individual situation.

Part Three, "Common Multipet Frustrations," explains some of the weird and wonderful cat foibles—why cats follow humans to the toilet— as well as the top behavior complaints of pet owners. You'll learn tips for dealing with scratching and countertop cruising, for example. Throughout the book, several running sidebars point out information of special interest.

Calming Signals offer the best bet tip from experts; **Comfort Zone** suggests helpful pet products; and the scary cat icon **Vet Alert!** warns you about situations that need expert help.

Part Four, "Appendices" lists the expert sources who provided information presented in this book. This includes professional animal behavior organizations for one-on-one help with your cat behavioral issues. I've also provided a "Further Information" section with activities and other resources that may prove helpful.

RISKY BUSINESS

Your cats' behavior problems can certainly be a challenge for you to deal with, but all too often they can lead to cats losing their lives. Shelters overflow with cats relinquished by owners fed up with what often is a "fixable" problem. Most of these fur-kids never get a second chance and end up losing their lives. This book can help you resolve a large percentage of behaviors and preserve the loving bond you share with your pets. Advice must be interpreted correctly, though. For instance, it can be difficult to figure out which cat baptized the drapes so you can apply those recommendations to the right feline.

Certain kinds of aggression have far reaching consequences, and prove challenging to even the most savvy professional. Aggression not only puts Sheba's life on the line, it risks other cats, dogs, and people and becomes a liability issue for you. Because of the smaller size, cat bites cause fewer reported injuries than bites from dogs but still can cause severe injury and dangerous infection. Anytime your pet has caused wounds in another pet or person that require medical care, you will need help beyond the scope of this book. Refer to the Appendix for how to find animal behavior consultants for help.

If you diligently follow the tips outlined in ComPETability but see no progress—or you feel so frustrated that you want to scream at your pet— yell for a professional instead. Individual people and pets absorb information in different ways and speeds, and a demonstration by a veterinary behaviorist or using a behavior modification program under the direction of an expert consultant may help you better understand the tips in this book, save your sanity, and preserve the love you share with your special cats.

USING THIS BOOK

It's not always easy to find the best way to present information so that it's understandable, accessible, and covers all the bases. A challenge with this three-book ComPETability series has been presenting parallel advice for both dog-to-dog and dog-to-cat issues and I've tried to avoid repetition as much as possible when it applies to both. Also, if you're like me, it offends you to have a pet referred to as "it," yet it can be awkward to say "he/she" over and over. For convenience's sake, the books typically refer to dogs as "he" and cats as "she" (but advice applies to both genders unless otherwise stated), and uses the generic pet names "Rex" for dogs and "Sheba" for cats.

The P.E.T. Test

Throughout the book you'll find references to the P.E.T. Test, an acronym designed to help you figure out the "why" behind a problem behavior. I've used this in many of my articles and books because it's an easy way to figure out what's going on. The acronym stands for **P**hysical Health, **E**motional Well-Being, and **T**raits Of Instinct. Only by knowing what triggers a "bad" behavior can you devise a plan to address the situation.

PHYSICAL HEALTH: Sick cats tell you they feel awful by behaving badly. Pain of any kind can make cats lash out, and cats suffering from hyperthyroidism typically display aggression or hyperactivity. Older pets can develop kidney failure that prompts indoor accidents when the cat can't reach her litter box. Any sudden change in behavior should be a wakeup call to get your pet checked by the veterinarian to rule out a physical health cause. A complete evaluation with blood tests and metabolic screening may be necessary to find subtle problems causing a change in personality or behavior, but when you can identify and treat these illnesses, the behavior problem usually goes away.

EMOTIONAL WELL-BEING: It's impossible to separate emotions from the physical realm. The stress of a new dog coming into Sheba's home can make her scratch-mark the sofa to feel more secure. Your old cat's fear of the new rambunctious kitten or a visiting toddler prompts hit-and-miss litter box lapses. Upset feelings can prompt overeating, or snubbing dinner. Negative emotions not only make cats unhappy, they also make cats succumb to illness more easily and take longer to recover. Unhappiness makes them more reactive to the other animals in the home, which can cause a cascade effect that sends your whole furry family into a meltdown. When your veterinarian has ruled out a physical problem, an emotional issue may have prompted the bad behavior.

TRAITS OF INSTINCT: Cats are born with certain inherent tendencies that make them behave in proscribed ways. Cats scratch the furniture to mark territory, and avoid a litter box that's not up to cleanliness standards. They don't act out to be "bad" or get back at you for some imagined slight—they can't help themselves and are doing what comes naturally. You can't change instinct but you can help your cats learn to redirect these behaviors into more acceptable actions—scratching a post instead of the sofa.

The L.E.A.S.H. Technique

An important part of living with more than one cat is to understand the dynamics of interactions to increase the odds for success. Proper introductions are the single most important step you can take, to ensure your pets will get along or even become fast friends. Depending on their age, breed, and history, cats want different things, and the chapters on cat-to-cat introductions detail step by step tips for various scenarios.

Before those whisker-to-whisker meetings, though, take some time to consider what your resident cats would like. After all, Sheba is already an important part of your family and just because YOU have fallen in love with a furry waif at the shelter doesn't mean your long time furry loves will welcome him with open paws.

If you want to adopt a particular cat breed, invest in a feline encyclopedia for an overview of their various care needs and personalities. Then visit at least one (more is better!) cat show. Speak frankly with the breeders and exhibitors and ask for guidance choosing the best fit for your furry family.

The better the match, the smoother introductions go and the sooner you'll build a peaceable kingdom between all the pets in your home. Use the L.E.A.S.H. Technique to help make informed decisions about matchmaking the new pet to your existing clowder. The acronym stands for five considerations when choosing your new pet friend, and can also be used to evaluate current resident pets. It stands for Lineage, Environment, Age, Sexual Status, and Health.

LINEAGE: Lineage influences pedigreed cats more than the random bred beauties. Cat breeds have less variation in size, looks and personality than do dogs, but some are known to be more vocal (Siamese), sedate (Persian), or active (Somali). An acrobat cat may pester your resident geriatric feline half to death, while a twenty-pound Maine Coon could injure a tiny puppy. A larger, mature cat also may be better able to hold her own against a toddler or a dog, and it's not unusual for a feline to rule in a doggy home. At least one study documented that kittens sired by "friendly" fathers would be more likely to inherit a "friendly" gene. When a kitten's father willingly interacts with you, chances are his offspring also will be more confident.

ENVIRONMENT: Environment influences both the way introductions should be made, and how well the cats get along once in the home. How would you feel if a stranger moved into your one-bedroom apartment and demanded to share your bed, food, toilet and time with loved ones? Why are we surprised many cats object?

A good rule of "paw" is to have no more pets than you have bedrooms. You can fudge this rule if the cats have extra vertical space (cat trees, window perches, hiding places). Cats prefer the status quo, and must be persuaded to put up with more pets. Not enough space in the house raises stress levels. A "house of plenty" in terms of food, toys, potties and space offers fewer opportunities to argue over who owns what.

AGE: Age of the pets involved is vital. A kitten threatens a resident cat's social status less than one of the same age. Older cats may forgive kitten indiscretions more readily, and Sheba can train the baby before the little guy gets too big to buffalo.

SEXUAL STATUS: Sexual status and gender greatly impact how well cats get along—or won't. Spaying and neutering all the felines in the household goes a long way toward leveling the playing field. The worst aggressions occur between same-sex pairings, so pick a new cat of the opposite gender.

HEALTH: Health issues make everything else unimportant. A medical problem automatically lowers the social standing of a cat. An ill or elderly resident feline likely will lose top cat status to the healthy newcomer. Healthy cats commonly pick on a health-challenged pet, and the stress, change in routine, and upset in status may make these pets feel even worse. So when Sheba isn't healthy, delay introducing a new pet until she feels better or take steps to ensure the safety and quality of life for all the pets involved.

COM*PET*ABLE TOOL CHEST

A number of helpful commercial and homemade products are recommended throughout the book. The best ones engage one or more of your cats' senses to entice them to "do the right thing" without forcing the situation. An overview of some of my favorites follows with a short recap of where they can help you with your cats' behavior issues.

Touching Techniques

Touch can be pleasant or unpleasant, used as a reward (as in petting) or a deterrent that stops unacceptable behaviors.

- *Figure-8 harness or small-size dog H-harness and leash.* Beneficial for stress reduction as well as management situations. The leash can be used as a *drag line* the leashed cat tows behind as she moves around the house. That can entice fearful cats to chase and play with the dragged leash. It can also be used to stop the cat's aggressive movements toward another feline when the owner steps on the line.
- *Thundershirt for Cats.* This is a snug-fitting vest that comes in small, medium and large sizes. The product helps reduce stress.
- *Sticky Paws.* The double-sided tape product keeps cats away from forbidden locations such as furniture, countertops and plants, as well as prevents scratching of illegal targets. The sticky surface is unpleasant when a cat touches with a furry paw and tender toe fur is pulled.
- *The Scarecrow or Garden Ghost.* Commercial product examples of motion-activated sprinklers that can keep unwanted animals out of your yard.

Sound Help

Acute hearing can get cats into trouble when the noise from outside critters (or bugs in the walls) drives them crazy. Sound can be used to cover up scary noises. Music works to soothe upset emotions and can be an effective natural tranquilizer. Other sounds can be used to humanely interrupt poor behavior.

- *Harp music* has a natural sedative effect; in people it has been shown to relieve pain. Harp music lowers the heart rate and blood pressure, slows respiration, increases the release of natural pain relievers (endorphins) and naturally calms pets.
- *Pet Melodies* and similar products are designed specifically for pets. Music can be therapeutic because the heart rhythm and brain waves tend to mimic (entrain) the tempos. Slow and soft music soothes and calms while faster music with a driving rhythm energizes. Music that your cat associates with you also can have a soothing influence.
- *Noise machines* create "white noise" that covers up distracting or unpleasant sounds that can be scary to cats. You can make your own white noise machine by tuning your radio to static.
- *The SSSCAT* cat-repellent device sprays a hiss of air when motion triggers the built-in detector. The sound startles and interrupts cats away from illegal areas. This booby-trap type product works particularly well since owners do not need to be present for it to work, and therefore the cats don't blame owners for the interruption.
- *Air horns* available in sports supply stores work well for breaking up cat fights without you risking your own injury.

Smelly Tips

Cats interact with their world through their noses. Scent can reward good behavior, and it can prevent bad behaviors or teach new ways of interacting.

- *Catnip* is a wonderful feline training tool. This harmless herb is a member of the mint family. The volatile oil is released when crushed by the cat biting or rolling on it, and acts like a cat hallucinogen to reduce feline inhibitions and shyness. About one-third of cats do not react to catnip (this is an inherited trait) but for those that do, catnip can be an important trick in the tool chest. For instance, catnip spiked on new cat trees helps teach cats to scratch the right object. Catnip also can calm cats during introductions. Use only once a week or the effect can wear off.

- *Pleasant scents* like your perfume or vanilla extract can be applied to all the cats to help them smell more alike. Since cats identify friendly family members by shared scent, this shortcut may help in some situations by dabbing a bit under the chin or back of the neck.
- *Citrus odors* tend to be off-putting to cats. Orange or lemon scents sprayed on forbidden furniture help keep cats away. Citrus peels scattered in the garden may shoo away stray cats.
- *Menthol odors* like Vicks also can repel pets and can be applied to illegal chew or scratch targets. You also can apply to a cloth and drape over the forbidden target.

Cleaning Potty Smells

Cats and dogs can detect minute chemical scents humans can't fathom. Simply mopping up the mess may satisfy your nose, but the smell lures pets back to the scene of the crime to repeat the dirty deed, time after time. Urine soaked into carpet proves particularly difficult to remove. With fresh accidents, pick up the solids and blot up as much liquid as possible. Avoid using ammonia based cleaning products. Since urine has ammonia in it, such products may mimic the smell and make the area even more attractive as a potty spot.

Once urine dries on carpet or walls, "pee-mail" notes are even more difficult to locate and clean. Turn off all your lights and shine a high-quality black light on suspect areas--that makes urine glow in the dark. Don't forget to check vertical areas such as walls and bedspreads that spraying cats and leg-lifting dogs like to target.

The best products don't just clean the area or cover up with perfumes, but actually neutralize the chemicals that smell bad. Urine is composed of sticky urea, urochrome (the yellow color), and uric acid. The first two can be washed away, but uric acid is nearly impossible to dissolve and remove from surfaces.

That's why successful products not only clean away the urea and urochrome, they also neutralize the uric acid with enzymes or encapsulate the urine molecules to contain the odor. Here are a few examples I've found to be successful and/or other professionals and colleagues have recommend to me. Ask for them at pet products stores, your veterinarian, Target, Walmart and similar sources as well as online.

- *Anti-Icky-Poo* uses live bacteria to eliminate any organic material left behind by your pets.
- *AtmosKlear Odor Eliminator* developed for the automotive industry can be used straight or mixed with other cleaning preparations. It's recommended for pet odors and other household odors (smoke, gym bags, basement mustiness, etc.).
- *Petastic* formerly known as Nature's Miracle, has been recommended by pet professionals for years. It employs an enzyme that breaks down and neutralizers the odor.
- *PetroTech Odor Eliminator* is made from organic ingredients that "encapsulate" the odors. I saw a demonstration of this product being sprayed into a cup of straight ammonia--and the odor disappeared instantly. This product claims to be safe for use on "skunked" pets, too.
- *Urine-Off* employs an enzyme that digests the urine molecules. The website also offers quality black lights for aid in finding and cleaning problem spots.
- *Zero Odor* is not an enzyme, but is composed of anti-odor molecules that bind with odor molecules and change them from smelly to non-offensive.

Eye On The Prize

Cats love to watch movement. Providing them with visual entertainment goes a long way toward keeping them out of trouble.

- *Bird feeders* or *bird baths* positioned directly outside windows keep cats' attention for hours. That decreases boredom and emotional upset.
- *Video Catnip* or other video products offer footage of fluttering birds, swimming fish, chattering squirrels and other critters. Indoor cats are most likely to enjoy watching kitty TV. Cats that have experienced the real thing may be more blasé.

Separate But Equal

Introductions, training sessions and sometimes daily living require cats to be separated. It's not necessary to segregate large areas, either.

- *Cat containment systems* like Cat Fence-In (www.catfencein.com) attaches fine webbing to existing outdoor fences to keep cats safely inside while allowing them to enjoy the outdoors. Purr…fect Fence (www.purrfectfence.com) also offers a complete backyard fence enclosure. Affordable Cat Fence (www.catfence.com) receives positive marks as well. All three offer do-it-yourself kits.
- *Cat tunnels* are great fun for cats and also offer hidden pathways for shy or fearful cats to navigate without the bully cats clobbering them. Tunnels are particularly helpful during introductions.
- *Second story property* is anything that allows the cats to get up off the floor level. Cat trees, window perches, and even the backs of tall sofas or an empty bookcase can provide the elevation cats seek. Homemade options might include creating a kitty gym from a wooden ladder decorated with suspended cat toys and a bed on the fold-out paint rack.
- *Baby gates* segregate pets during introductions, help retraining and provide boundaries. A variety of styles are available, some designed specifically for pets. Cats often can leap over standard issue gates, but you can stack them in doorways to keep high-altitude cats behind the barrier.
- *Pet doors* also offer great options for providing access to specific rooms inside the home, or outdoor availability to a porch or cat-safe back yard. Electronic pet doors can be programmed to only allow specified cats access if they wear the right collar or have the correct microchip. Pets without this "key" cannot pass through.

Playtime Games

Toys not only entertain, interactive games teach cats confidence, reduce shyness and helps them associate positive fun things with you and the other cats. Toys also reduce boredom and give cats legal outlets for racing around, clawing and biting.

- *Fishing pole toys* and other chase and lure toys build on the predatory instinct for cats to chase and capture. Many commercial versions of these "cat tease" toys are available. You can also find feathers for supervised games from craft stores for less cost than those available at pet products outlets or cat shows.

- *Flashlight beams and laser lights* can be great fun for some cats to chase. Be aware that some cats can develop obsessions with the elusive light, so teach Sheba that the light always appears and disappears in the same place (a cabinet drawer or the tip of your shoe). That way they know the game is over and learn to stop pestering you. Avoid shining any light in the cat's eyes, as that can injure vision.

- *Puzzle toys* keep cats occupied and their brains engaged in something productive. They can be filled with a portion of the cats' regular food or with special treats. Puzzle toys for cats work especially well for bored cats or those suffering from separation anxiety behaviors. A wide range of puzzle toys and interactive feeders are now available specifically for cats. You can also make a puzzle toy by filling an empty water bottle with kibble (lid off) so the cat must knock it around to shake out the food.

"ComPETability" offers a simple message: You can do more for your cats' happiness and health—and your own peace of mind—than you think. Pet love is a lifelong adventure, filled with chills, spills, and more than a few furry thrills. So, if you're ready to double, triple, even quadruple your fun, enjoy the ride! You won't be sorry.

Chapter 2
HOW CATS THINK

Humans have shared their laps with cats since the days of ancient Egypt, and while they command our respect and we cherish their grace, devotion to loved ones, and wild child perspective, we still fall short in understanding how Sheba thinks. Feline behavior "problems" typically reflect a human misunderstanding of normal cat needs, and adding to your kitty quotient increases the potential for problems.

Cats challenge our patience when they claw the sofa, "water" the potted palm, and throw hissy fits with other cats. People unfamiliar with them perpetuate the myth that cats are untrainable, independent creatures that "walk alone" and prefer solitary lifestyles. While cats are territorial, they are also social animals who enjoy contact with the special people and pets in their lives. But Sheba picks her friends carefully, so owners and other cats and dogs must meet on her terms, to earn full affection and cooperation. Once you learn how to communicate with and understand the feline mind, your relationship will improve by leaps and pounces. Your purrfect pet partnership awaits!

LEARNING TO BE A CAT

Kittens aren't born knowing the rules of feline behavior, and instead must learn the proper c'attitudes by both observation and experience. Earliest cat lessons are taught by Sheba's mom-cat, and she won't understand human expectations without proper instructions from you.

Kittens with the worst genetic roll of the dice can develop a wonderful personality with the proper teachers. Conversely, the ideal kitten personality can turn hissy if she learns the wrong thing. Everything that Sheba experiences influences her behavior—even accidental lessons you never intend to teach. Understanding how kittens and cats learn helps you be the best feline teacher possible, so that they play by your rules and you understand theirs.

The Feline Family

Kittens inherit a lot from cat parents, including looks, instincts, and even personality tendencies. Both parent personality and health play a crucial role in determination of a cat's future behavior. Kittens born of "friendly" fathers tend to inherit "boldness," a positive response to unfamiliar or novel objects. The bold kitty meets life head on, and has less overall stress-related health issues as compared to shy/fearful cats. Studies also show that kittens of undernourished mothers have less ability to learn, and display more antisocial behavior towards other cats. Even if these kittens are fed enough later in life, some of these deficits will be passed onto the next generation of kittens.

While there are more similarities among cats, researchers speculate that some differences in behavior may correlate to looks inherited from parents. Coat coloring pigments (melanin) are produced by the same biochemical pathway in the brain as dopamine, a substance that plays an important role in brain activity, and hence, coat color may influence behavior. One study suggested that cats carrying the non-agouti allele—a type of gene that produces solid coat colors (usually black cats)—may be more tolerant of crowding and the conditions of urban life, as well as having a greater amicability. In other words, black cats may adjust more readily to living in groups of felines.

In the early days of experimental psychology, adult cats often were used as subjects in studies of learning. Felines quickly discovered how to escape from puzzle boxes with novel kinds of fasteners, but couldn't learn by trial and error the concept of pressing a lever to receive food—something pigeons quickly mastered! In modern experiments, researchers found that kittens who watched mom press a lever to get food quickly learned to perform the trick when they had a role model. Kittens watching their own mom learned more quickly than if they watched a strange female cat, so learning improves if the "mentor" is familiar. This illustrates that cats aren't well suited to learning monotonous tasks, but like a challenge and model behavior by example. Sheba evolved to out-think smart prey that hides in ever-changing locations.

Cats exhibit two major personality types: sociable/confident/trusting, and timid/nervous/shy. The "independent" cats further may be categorized as alert, social and equable (not overly emotional one way or another). While you can't control what your cat inherited, you can help promote positive nurturing with training. The very smartest cats know they are smarter than you are, and prove to be challenges to train—yet may feign being "slow" simply to get away with murder. Understanding the basics of feline learning better prepares you to stay a step ahead of your cats and enhance your relationship.

CALMING SIGNALS: TEMPERAMENT TESTS

Puppies more commonly receive temperament tests to try and predict adult dog personality and tendencies. While this is not an exact science, it can help owners better predict the future so they can choose appropriate matches during adoption. Some of the same puppy temperament test techniques apply to kittens.

- Pick up the kitten and set on your lap, and pet her. Does she tolerate the touch or seem to enjoy the attention? Or does she immediately struggle to escape, and even scratch, bite or hiss?
- Test the kitten's timidity by dropping a book on the floor or jingling keys—something mildly startling. Does it cause her to jump but then settle? Or is she instantly fearful with attempts to escape or hide? How long does it take for her to recover?
- Offer a smelly, tasty treat right in front of the kitten. Most kittens (except immediately after a meal) should willingly sniff and taste or even munch the treat even in front of strangers. Kittens that refuse

a tasty treat may indicate the potential for being more easily stressed or fearful in new circumstances.

Kitten Kindergarten

Cats learn all their lives but are virtual sponges from two to seven weeks of age during what's termed the prime socialization period. This narrow window during babyhood prepares kittens for the rest of their lives; however, learning the "wrong" lessons can emotionally cripple the pet. If they are not exposed to positive experiences with humans during this socialization period, kittens act similarly to wild animals unable to easily accept people as safe.

During this time, kittens develop feline social and communication skills while learning to identify acceptable and unacceptable members of their family. Mother cats teach these skills through example. Babies learn to use a litter box by following Mom-Cat to the facilities. If the mother gets hissy around dogs, her kittens copy the behavior. This helps socialize the baby so that the kittens will later "generalize" this response and react positively to other people, too.

Kittens separated too early from maternal and sibling interactions develop poor social bonds later in life. Kittens have more confidence when they are accompanied by Mom-cat and siblings, and socializing them with both will reduce anxiety. Littermates and the mother cat also teach claw and bite limits and how to inhibit both.

Hand-raised kittens tend to become overly rambunctious and less inhibited with their teeth and claws. Ideally, kittens should stay with Mom and littermates at least until 12-16 weeks of age. People raising kittens must socialize them before the babies go to new homes. Once the baby arrives in her new home, owners should strive for a positive outcome in new situations and continue to provide exposure to a variety of people (men, women, children), places (home, grandma's, the vet), and novel situations and objects to explore.

To promote a trusting relationship and a confident cat, begin by creating a kitten kindergarten, teaching the Three T's —**Touching, Talking,** and **Timing.**

TOUCHING: The more you touch a kitten, the "friendlier" she will be towards humans. Studies have shown that handling furry babies for five minutes a day during their first three weeks increases the pet's ability to learn later in life. Fifteen minutes of loving touch a day helps enormously, but about 45 minutes a day during the sensitive period is ideal. Being handled by several people (including kids) helps her be more accepting of multiple individuals. Touching the youngster not only feels good to you both, it teaches her that contact with people is pleasant, not scary, and self-rewarding. Touch also places your scent on her, so she associates your smell with good feelings. Petting comforts kittens because it hearkens back to one of the first sensations newborns feel when Mom licks and grooms them. In addition, your pleasant touch prompts a reduction in blood pressure and heart rate, causing a positive change in brain wave activity.

TALKING: Talking to the youngster teaches her to listen and pay attention to your voice. Kittens may not understand all the words, but will recognize if you're happy, aggravated, amused, or affectionate. Make a point of using your cats' names when you speak to them in a positive way: "What a lovely smart Sheba! Scratching the right object, good Sheba!" That helps a cat learn to associate her name with good things related to you. The more you speak to your cats, the better they learn to understand and react to what you want.

TIMING: Timing is the third "T" and extremely important when you understand that kittens have the attention span of a four-year-old toddler. If you find claw marks on the Persian rug, and drag Sheba to the scene of the crime, she won't have a clue why you're angry. You must catch her in the act—or within 30 seconds of the behavior—for her to associate your displeasure with what she's done. When training, praise always works better than punishment and you'll get better results by catching her in the act of scratching the RIGHT object. Reward good behaviors immediately, with praise, a treat or favorite toy. Use timing to your advantage, and your cats will look for ways to please you.

The "Whoops" Effect

A "whoops" experience can be a happy accident or create behavior problems down the road. Kittens and cats continue to learn an incredible amount through observation, even after the prime socialization period ends. A friendly, trusting cat needs only a few positive interactions with a strange person to show positive behavior toward them, and it takes significant negative experiences to override this initial response. On the contrary, a shy cat needs LOTS of positive experiences with a stranger to overcome lack of socialization during the sensitive phase, and will react adversely toward even minor negative encounters.

In other words, the socialized cat generalizes positive experiences quickly, but the unsocialized cat must learn gradually to trust the individual person or family and does NOT generalize later positive experiences. Instead she expects that one negative experience will apply to all new situations.

When your current cat(s) know good manners, they serve as wonderful role models to new pets. By observing your interaction with a resident cat that meows at a certain time each day to get fed, Sheba more quickly makes that connection. Think of this as a positive "copycat" behavior. New cats also learn bad habits from a resident feline and vice versa. If you allow Sheba to get away with wild antics, the older cat also may start pushing your buttons. Adult cats learn by watching you, too. After seeing you open a door, they learn to jump up and hang on the door 'lever' to open it.

Cats are experts at getting their way. They are so good at training owners, that we often don't recognize we are being manipulated. Sheba easily trains you to fill the food bowl when she paw-pats you awake you at 5:30 a.m. It only takes one or two repetitions of this cause-and-effect for cats to remember what works in each situation. If rattling the wooden window blinds makes you let her out the door, she'll remember and use that ploy again and again. Therefore, pay attention to not only what Sheba does, but your own resulting behavior, to get a clue how she's training you.

There are times when our patience runs out, and owners may be tempted to react with anger. To be blunt, corporeal punishment doesn't work. Hitting, yelling, or using force not only is inhumane, it almost always makes the bad behavior worse. Dr. Gary Lansberg, a veterinary behaviorist, explains that any strong arousal interferes with Sheba's ability to learn because that portion of the brain must deal with the emotional fallout instead. Instead of thinking, these cats react out of instinct (the fight-or-flight response) and typically either attack, or hide. You'll teach a lesson you don't want Sheba to learn—to fear or dislike you.

SPEAKING FELINESE

Cat language consists of a complex system of vocalization, scent signals, and body postures, which define and reinforce the cat's social position within the family group. While we can't "read" the odiferous messages, cats give us clear postures and vocal signals about their intentions, and ignoring these warnings can get you bit.

Signals can be divided into those that seek to decrease the distance between individuals or that warn you to increase the distance. Cats use their ears, tail, fur, eyes, and every part of their body to "talk." To understand felinese, pay attention not only to the individual body parts, but to the entire repertoire, or you risk misunderstanding Sheba's message. In multiple cat homes, understanding what your pets tell you—and what your own body language and vocal tone tells them—means the difference between a happy home and chaos. Learn the basics to translate cat language into people-speak.

Cat Calls

Cats are one of the most vocal of carnivore species, says Sharon L. Crowell-Davis, DVM, a behaviorist at the College of Veterinary Medicine, University of Georgia. Behaviorists describe sixteen distinct feline vocal patterns that fall under four general categories: murmur patterns include purrs and trills; vowel patterns are meows in all their variations (cats can produce several diphthongs, too); articulated patterns are chirps and chattering that express frustration; and strained intensity patterns are warnings such as hisses and growls, or shrieks of pain. Both males and females use strained intensity patterns in sexual communication. The abruptness or volume of the pain shriek may also be designed to shock or startle the attacker to loosen the grip. Experts also speculate that some cat vocalizations may be so subtle or pitched at such a frequency, that only cats can hear these "silent meows."

Cat communication begins early in life. Kittens less than three weeks old vocalize a defensive spit, contented purr, and distress call (similar to adult meow) if the baby becomes isolated, cold, or trapped. Interestingly, the call for "cold" sounds much higher pitched,and disappears from the repertoire once the kitten can self-regulate body temperature at about four weeks of age. Cats rarely meow at each other. They learn to direct meows at humans because we reward them with attention. Each cat learns by association that meowing prompts feeding, access to locations, and other resources provided by humans. Some cats learn to produce unique meows for each circumstance.

The purr, on the other hand, is more complex and something that we still don't completely understand. Kittens purr almost from birth, causing some experts to speculate that the infant's purr tells the mother all is well with the baby, or solicits contact/care, and that adult cats retain this infantile trait once they grow up.

Purrs arise on both inhale and exhale of breath in a continuous unbroken sound. The sudden build-up and release of pressure creates the sound as the glottis alternately opens and closes to cause a sudden separation of the vocal folds. The laryngeal muscles move the glottis to generate this cycle every 30 to 40 milliseconds. Purring almost always takes place in the presence of another person or cat, and another theory suggests that purring acts as a calming signal to declare to others, "I am no threat." While we usually associate purring with contentment, cats also purr when in pain or frightened, and some purr as they die. The vibration associated with purring has been shown to help speed healing, and may function as a unique self-healing benefit.

Kitty Post-It Notes

The ancestral cat hunted and lived alone, and like other animals that don't routinely meet face to face, modern cats still communicate with scent. Scent messages allow a delay of hours to days between a cat's deposit of the scent and another feline's sniffing of it, so encounters with rivals can be avoided based on scent signals.

"The cat's sense of smell is 1000 times stronger than ours," says Bruce D. Elsey, DVM, a feline practice veterinarian, and because today pet cats don't live the same lifestyle as wild cousins, feline scent communication may have modified through domestication. Evidence of this lies in the theory that cats living in groups produce colony or group specific odors.

These group odors develop when cats groom each other, cheek- body-rub one another (called allorubbing) and sleep together, says Dr. Crowell-Davis. Skin glands located on the chin, lips, cheeks, forehead, tail and paws produce the "name tag" scent that individually identifies one cat from another. Friendly cats rub their tails against each other's bodies and twine their tails together. Face rubbing (bunting) not only marks the target as "owned" by the kitty, it may be a subtle sign of deference with the subordinate feline approaching and bunting the more dominant pet or person.

GROOMING BEHAVIOR

Grooming not only keeps cats looking spiffy, it spreads the individual cat's scent throughout the fur and helps maintain healthy skin. The massage action of cat tongues stimulates the production of sebum, an oily secretion produced by sebaceous glands at the base of each hair, and licking spreads sebum over the hair coat to lubricate and waterproof the fur, and make it shine. It also removes loose hair and prevents mats, and removes dirt and parasites like fleas.

Grooming is a barometer of feline health. Emotional or physical illness may trigger excessive grooming behavior such as licking a painful area bald.

Displacement Grooming

Cats also groom as an emotional release. Behaviors that seem inappropriate to the situation are termed "displacement" behaviors. Cats use grooming in this function more than any other behavior. Your kitty may suddenly groom herself when feeling fearful, to relieve tension, or when uncertain how to react to a situation.

For example, an aggressive interaction may be followed with a bout of frantic self-grooming to soothe the stress. A classic example of displacement grooming appears when a cat misjudges a leap and falls—and then begins to furiously groom as though embarrassed.

Self-grooming as a displacement behavior helps the cat deal with conflict. Perhaps the touch-sensation has a direct effect on the brain chemistry or neurologic impulses that make the distressed cat feel better. In other words, self-grooming may be self-medicating with a feline form of Prozac. It may also serve to lower body temperature that elevates due to stress. Or maybe it's just an unconscious way for the cat to distract herself, the way some people bite their nails to relieve tension.

Mutual Grooming

Grooming each other (allogrooming) not only spreads communal scent, it also serves as a clue about which cat rules the roost, and how your cats prefer to be petted by you. Mutual grooming targets the head and neck, and the recipient usually cooperates with head tilts and purring. Dominant cats groom less dominant ones more often and allogrooming can sometimes be a form of redirected aggression or dominance behavior.

Besides helping a cat buddy with a hard-to-reach spot, mutual grooming demonstrates a friendly relationship between cats. Mutual grooming is more of a social activity than a hygienic one. Grooming another cat expresses comfort, companionship, and even love. Cats that groom an owner's hair, lick your arm, and accept the owner's petting actually are engaging in mutual grooming that expresses utmost trust and affection.

Pheromone Communication

Other kitty Post-It Notes arise from the scent glands located between the pads of the paws. Sheba deposits scent when she scratches and this doubles as a visual marker that communicates to other felines the property is owned. Notice where your cat prefers to scratch to figure out the best position for cat trees and other legal scratch objects you provide. Cats target scratch sites distributed along regularly used routes—the path between the front window and the food bowl—rather than at the periphery of the territory or home range. That's why Sheba ignores the post hidden away in a back room.

In addition to smells, cats detect and react to pheromones, species-specific chemicals that animals naturally produce. "Pheromones are a type of chemical communication between animals," says Marie-Laure Loubiere, DVM, a veterinarian involved in pheromone research with CEVA Sante Animal S.A., in France.

Researcher Daniel Mills, BVSc, PhD, says scent detection is very different from pheromone communications. Odors must be analyzed in the cortex, the "thinking" portion of the brain. "That's what we call cognition," he says. The cat learns what an individual scent means, and associates the tuna odor with a memory of its taste.

Pheromones have nothing to do with learned memory. The limbic system of the brain perceives pheromone information directly, and no thinking takes place—the brain automatically recognizes the message.

"Pheromones change the behavior without having to involve the cortex," says Dr. Mills. Kittens understand the meaning from birth, even before their eyes or ears open. Cats rely on this specialized natural pheromone communication all their lives, using the pheromones produced in skin glands and urine to understand what other kitties mean.

Urine contains pheromones used in marking/territorial communication (sort of a "pee-mail" message), and also announces the sexual status of the cat who sprays. Spraying of an intact male cat helps suppress the sexual behavior of less dominant cats that venture in that territory, while intact female cats spray to announce their breeding receptivity. Pheromones that arise from the cats' cheeks also serve as marking tools to "label" territory as known and safe, as well as identify individuals as friendly/no threat. Pheromones also have been identified that are produced from mammary tissue that serves to reduce fearfulness in kittens during nursing.

Body Talk

Cats have a wide range of body postures used as visual signals primarily to regulate aggressive behavior. Determining the meaning of a signal or group of signals depends on context, and what the rest of the body says. Rolling, for example, is a component of female sexual behavior, usually accompanied by purring, stretching, and kneading interspersed with object-rubbing bouts. But when an immature male cat rolls in the presence of a dominant male, the behavior signals appeasement, and says, "I'm no threat, treat me nice." Neutered cats (both male and female) use rolling behavior toward humans as an appeasement gesture, and sometimes as an invitation to interact or play.

Similarly, the tail can be an important indicator of a cat's mood. Kittens greet mom-cat with tail-up posture, and adult cats use "tail up" directed at humans or other cats to say, "I come in friendship." One cat may signal from across the room and then approach when the other kitty returns the friendly gesture. Conversely, the tail wrapped around the body is a distance-increasing gesture that tells others to stay away.

In any situation (offensive, defensive, or relaxed), cats control space from a distance with stares. During the preliminary stages of tense encounters, they may avoid looking at each other, but eventually the dominant cats will use long-distance stares to keep other cats away from owned property (such as a litter box).

As aggression increases, more overt signs develop. An aggressive cat fluffs her fur (piloerection) and stands at full height. Ears are barometers of kitty mood. Erect, forward-facing ears indicate interest, but the more of the backs of the ears she shows, the greater her agitation and threat to attack. Lashing of the tail from side to side also indicates arousal. "Cats don't do submission," says Dr. Patricia Pryor, a veterinary behaviorist at Washington State University. They communicate fear or non-contest by crouching on ground, flattening ears and withdrawing head into the shoulders. Gauge kitty fearfulness by the degree to which the ears flatten.

Let the Games Begin

Play reaches its peak by age 9 to 16 weeks, and declines thereafter. While adult cats tend to fall into the "playful" or "lap sitter" categories, all felines continue to play to a certain extent. Play behavior in cats can be described as locomotory, social, and object oriented. Running, jumping, rolling and climbing (locomotory) can be done "solo" or be interactive with others.

Object play involves the cat targeting anything from a bug to a feather and turning it into a toy. Social play means cats interact with each other or owners, and can include wrestling, biting, pouncing, play-fighting, and chase-tag games.

Behaviors for fighting and fun are similar, and you need to recognize the difference, as play fighting can escalate to aggression and require a human referee. Cats exaggerate fighting postures to indicate play, or the sequences may be jumbled. They may roll on the ground to invite play, "hop," or tippy-toe sideways with fluffed fur, or bring a toy and drop it nearby. On occasion cats will race past another cat and whop him with a paw as a drive-by invitation to play tag. During wrestling games, cats use inhibited bites and retracted claws. In these instances of appropriate play, all the cats willingly participate and take turns chasing each other.

Inappropriate play results in one or more cat frightened, hurt, or overwhelmed. Mouthing aimed primarily at the back of the neck, or uninhibited bites means play has gotten out of hand. You'll hear hisses or screams from the bitten cat. Vocalizations are rare during cat play, so if one or both cats get noisy, or repeatedly attempts to get away, separate them to see if they go back for more.

Feline Poker

Cats use a variety of dominant postures and avoidance behaviors to either bluff their way into positions of authority, or to cry uncle and fold their cards without losing face. They interact in such subtle ways it can be easy to miss these feline "conversations." Pay attention to the following body signals to understand if one cat seeks to rule the roost, or to just "get along" by appeasing feline housemates. Keep in mind, though, that while Sheba may be dominant in the TV room, another cat often "rules" other locations. A dominant cat:

- Maintains eye contact, and stares to control space
- Rotates ears forward
- Holds head high, with erect, tense and rigid posture (standing on tippy toes)
- Fluffs fur all over her body (piloerection)
- Grasps other cat by the nape of the neck (inhibited bite)
- "Power grooms" other cat (aggression may follow)

Once you understand what Sheba says, it improves your relationship. Use the signals yourself—averting your eyes, or turning your head away— to calm a fearful kitty. Offer your fist for the cat to sniff, because some cats react to this as though to another cat's round head that "bunts" to signal no threat. Other common feline appeasement gestures include:

- Play bowing (with front legs motionless)
- Sitting, with back to other cat/you
- Crouching
- Repeated rolling
- Yawning
- Nose touching
- Approaching with tail up

THE PHYSICAL CAT

Feline behavior and health directly impact each other. A behavior change commonly indicates a health problem but cats may continue the misbehavior (for example, miss the litter box) long after the physical problem (constipation) has resolved. Cats hide discomfort extremely well, but may bite or claw in response to petting that inadvertently hurts them.

Feline Form and Function

All felines remain amazingly similar in size, function, and personality, but many can be categorized into two very broad body and behavior types based on how they evolved. The oldest breeds arose spontaneously as a result of their environment, and major differences are coat length and body conformation.

The "warm weather" body type (Oriental) like the Siamese arose in the temperate climates of Asia, and is characterized by lithe, muscular cats with long, lean legs, whip like tails, large ears, slanting eyes, longish muzzle and thin single coat. These cats tend to be vocal, active, swing-from-the-drapes-type cats. The "cold weather" body type (cobby), typified by the Persian appeared in the colder climates of Europe, and have short, square, compact bodies with a broad head, small ears, short muzzle, round eyes, and a thick weather-resistant double coat. These cats often are sedate, quiet, lap-snugglers.

Feline design ideally suits the cats' ultimate purpose as predators of small game, whether she weighs 4 to 6 pounds (as in the Singapura) or is a heavyweight like the 20-plus pound Maine Coon. Cats hunt by stalk and pounce, using bursts of energy to explode upon unsuspecting prey. They use paws like hands and paw-pat everything before trusting it in their mouths. Adult cats kill quickly and efficiently with a bite to back of neck that severs the spinal cord. For pet cats, of course, the victim most often is catnip mice and stuffed feather toys. Give Sheba a legal outlet for her energy by providing regular exercise to keep muscles toned, body healthy, and mind active.

Cat Senses Explained

Feline senses are much more acute than our own, and cats rely on eyesight much more than dogs do. They expertly detect movement from peripheral vision, need only 1/6th the amount of light that people do, and use twice as much of the available light, enabling them to function in low-light conditions. If human eyes were proportionally the same size as the cats' our eyes would be eight inches across. When cats lose their vision due to cataracts, glaucoma or age, oftentimes they develop temporary behavior problems until they can adjust.

Scent communication between cats serves to identify family from stranger, and aids with social interactions. Besides their noses, the vomeronasal organ located between the soft palate and nasal passages reacts to pheromones, specialized chemicals that communicate directly to the cat's brain. Because cats rely so much on scent to determine food safety and stimulate appetite, a stuffy nose has dire health consequences.

More than scent or sight, cats rely on their ears, and hear sounds in a 10.5 octave range, a wider span of frequencies than almost any other mammal. This range allows her to detect extremely high frequencies and even ultrasonic squeals of mice. Since cats need this sense above all others, age, which increases the risk of deafness, can severely interfere with communication between cats or with their owners.

The feline sense of touch is most sensitive in the area surrounding the muzzle and on the paw pads. Each hair on Kitty's body originates deep in the skin, next to a nerve receptor sensitive to vibration, touch, heat, cold, and/or pain. Just brushing the tips of the whiskers, for instance, telegraphs information to Sheba about air movement, barometric pressure, petting or punishment. Over-stimulation—excessive petting—can prompt aggression in some cats.

Specific tastes vary between cats. Though they often share similar tastes as people, they don't detect the same sugar/sweet flavors, and instead are most attracted to meaty tastes. Strong-smelling treats can be a great training tool for food-motivated cats. That's one reason cats react so favorably to the pungent aroma of fishy canned foods.

Kittens, Juveniles, Adults, And Old Fogies

As kittens grow up and mature, their behavior evolves during each life stage. From five to seven weeks of age, the drive to copy Mom-cat becomes consuming, and babies learn to eat solid food, use the litter box, and play "nice" with peers. While adult cats may not care for them and avoid contact with furry infants, most recognize them as babies and rarely offer to harm youngsters.

Juvenile delinquent behavior develops during month three to six and can be aggravating for even laid-back adults. More confrontations between adults and delinquent kittens take place either because the adults want to teach manners, or the kittens haven't a clue and continue brainless behavior. While some adult cats of either gender (intact or neutered) take these teenage kittens under their paws and have great patience, more often the older feline avoids the miscreant or whips her furry tail into polite behavior.

According to Bonnie Beaver, DVM, a veterinary behaviorist at Texas A & M University, kittens are very social until they reach six to ten months of age when they experience a dramatic change in personality. Interactive play becomes rougher and tends to end with aggression. Over time the length of play bouts decreases, while aggression increases and becomes more intense. In a feral setting, this serves to disperse the littermates, but in a household, owners bear the brunt of rough interaction. The personality can't be changed back, but you can redirect aggressive play toward legal toys.

Conventional wisdom suggests cats reach adulthood by twelve months of age. However, bodies and coats continue to develop up to 24 months in certain breeds. Social maturity takes place between 2½ and four years of age, at which time these maturing cats may challenge older ones for a higher ranking in the social hierarchy. Cats age quite gracefully, and may not show age-related changes until they reach eight to ten years or older. Sensory or mobility challenges and other health issues often result in crotchety older cats' behavior changes.

Acting Romantic

For all cats, behavior is inseparable from sexuality. Kittens practice mounting, biting necks, clasping and thrusting during play, and adolescents continue to experiment as they mature. Male kittens often mount a variety of objects including pillows, blankets, other cats or even your arm. Mounting behavior between adult spayed or neutered cats often is a dominance display, and masturbation can be a way for a stressed kitty to calm himself down.

Oriental-type cats such as Siamese mature quite early, with girls sometimes able to become pregnant as early as four months of age. Females go in and out of season every 21 days, from about February through October, and theoretically could have up to three litters a year. Males mate as early as six to nine months. Hormone-related behaviors include female rolling, crying, and screaming during heat, spraying urine in marking behavior, roaming to find willing mates, and dominance displays that can evolve into aggression and fights.

Spaying removes the ovaries and uterus of female cats, while castration removes the testes of male cats. Both surgeries are referred to as neutering, and eliminate the chance of accidental babies. When performed prior to sexual maturity, neutering prevents or reduces many hormone-related behavior problems, so today, animal welfare societies often perform the surgery once pets reach two pounds, during kittenhood.

The Cat Clowder

Cat society defines how cats deal with each other. No longer thought of as antisocial loaners, today we know felines relate and interact with each other in dynamic and very fluid hierarchies. When enough food and other resources are present, adult females associate in lineages, which are the building blocks of cat society. Similar to lions, domestic kitties in colony settings may suckle each other's babies, sever umbilical cords, move kittens to new locations, and otherwise communally raise the infants.

Large cat colonies may have several such lineages. Each usually consists of related adult females and successive generations of their offspring. Females relate within their lineage and to a lesser extent outside of it. These tend to be friendly, well-integrated groups of cats, with the eldest female holding the highest status. Juveniles and kittens automatically become socially integrated to their birth lineage and these ties usually last a lifetime if the cats remain in each other's company. Ties of adult females to their sons and daughters are stronger than to nephews and nieces.

Most observation of free-living cats suggests that adult males rarely are affiliated with any one lineage, usually only temporarily during mating. However, cats in feral situations often choose to sit together, establish feline friendships, and each individual favors company of some over others. The age, sex, social status and blood ties of the individuals involved govern these associations.

Toms also are said not to be involved in kitten rearing, but Dr. Crowell-Davis says that's not always true. Intact toms have been seen helping queens defend kittens from invading toms, to groom babies, share food with juveniles, and to curl up around abandoned kittens. Males also sometimes disrupt intense wrestling play between juveniles, using a forelimb to separate them without using aggression against either.

Felines in any given family group—composed mostly of females with some immature males and the occasional Tom—offer a united front and show hostility toward strange cats that attempt to join the society. Non-group members are not allowed to casually approach and enter the group. If the unknown cat or kitten persists, they may eventually be integrated into the group but only over time that involves many interactions. Therefore, introducing a new cat into a resident cats' territory almost always proves challenging for owners. Introducing very young cats of the opposite sex into a resident adult's social group works best, as it offers the fewest social challenges to the dominant feline.

The feline social structure depends on a hierarchy of dominant and subordinate individuals. Rank of the individual cat decides which one gets the preferred access to valued resources: resting spots, food pans, water, toys, your attention, and so on.

Cats don't follow a clear linear hierarchy, though. There is usually an obvious top cat and one or two bottom cats (called pariahs because they get picked on by the others), but no number two, three, or four cats with stair-step ranking below the dominant feline. Instead, most cats share an equal "middle space." This more fluid social standing requires a decision about who eats first, crosses a path first, gets the best sleeping spot time after time, on a case-by-case basis, says Dr. Beaver. Sometimes the calico wins the day while the tabby gets her choice another time.

This time-share mentality allows every cat (even middle management) to feel like a King. Time-share means the cats don't need to fight over property. It may appear that one cat owns the second floor of your home, while another cat owns the family room. This makes perfect sense if you consider that people also bow to the whims of a boss while at work, but we call the shots in our own homes.

Subordinate cats signal deference by looking away, lowering ears slightly, turning the head away and leaning back when they encounter a cat dominant to them. Often close encounters are simply avoided by giving way spatially—the subordinate cat gets off the path, jumps off the chair, or otherwise acknowledges the other cat's right. Cat #1 may own the second floor, but when she's not around, Cat #2 lounges there with impunity—

timeshares the area because the first cat wasn't using it. When the owner returns, the subordinate cat pretends not to care, looks the other way (so he doesn't have his nose rubbed in it!) and relinquishes the territory when Cat #1 returns.

Dominant cats show their status with a direct stare, stiffening of the limbs, holding ears erect while turning them sideways, and elevating the base of the tail while the rest of it droops. The display usually prompts the subordinate cat to defer.

Fights occur most often during introductions of new cats into an existing feline society, or when a change in social status due to infirmity or maturing adolescent cats takes place. Ownership of property rates very highly among cats. When rare valued resources must be shared, the potential for arguments escalates. It's important for owners to acknowledge the dominant status of the highest-ranking cat (by feeding first), while providing enough resources for lower ranking cats (multiple litter boxes and feeding stations).

Chapter 3

PAWSITIVE PURRSUASION

Owners have long turned to dog trainers to teach Rex better manners, but until relatively recently, cats have gotten shortchanged. But of course savvy cat owners now recognize that Sheba also can be trained. It's helpful to briefly explain some of the complicated terms used by animal behaviorists for better understanding of some of the book recommendations.

Classical conditioning introduced by Pavlov and his bell-ringing dog-drooling experiments is one tool. He showed that an unconditioned trigger (such as food) prompts an unconditioned/unlearned response (salivation). More importantly, Pavlov showed that neural stimuli, such as a bell, once associated with the uncontrolled stimuli (food) prompts a conditioned reflex. This technique teaches dogs and cats to learn, or become conditioned to, a sound, smell or behavior associated with a particular response.

Operant conditioning, introduced by B.F. Skinner's box experiments, prompted rats to learn to press a lever to get food pellets. Operant conditioning deals with relationships between stimuli, responses, and consequences. The pet learns that what he does (sit on command) is critical to what happens next (gets a food reward).

"Behavior modification seeks to get the desirable versus punish the undesirable," says Dr. Lansberg. You do that through the use of various types of reinforcement and punishment. Punishment can either be "positive" or "negative" with varying results.

- POSITIVE PUNISHMENT: The word "positive" means you ADD something the pet doesn't like to get the desired results, and usually causes some degree of fear in the pet. For example, the electric scat mat adds a shock to prevent Sheba jumping on the sofa, while hitting Sheba makes her stop climbing the drapes. Positive punishment that causes pain or fear has little to no place in modern training.
- NEGATIVE PUNISHMENT: The word "negative" means you REMOVE something that the pet likes, so a "good thing" goes away when the pet performs the undesirable behavior. For example, if the kitten bites during play, the game stops. Negative punishment can be used humanely and effectively.

Reinforcement refers to some sort of incentive that prompts the pet to want to perform a particular behavior. Different cats respond better to various reinforcers, but a special treat or toy—whatever floats the pet's boat—works best, particularly if you reserve it only for training. The cat only gets her favorite feather toy during training sessions, for example.

- POSITIVE REINFORCEMENT means the desired behavior results in ADDING something pleasant or positive. For example, a treat lures the cat to wave. To be effective, positive reinforcement must be contingent upon the desired behavior taking place; must be associated with the behavior; and must be used consistently.
- NEGATIVE REINFORCEMENT means the desired behavior results in the REMOVAL of something unpleasant or negative. For example, a frightened dog barks at the mailman, the mailman's departure negatively reinforces the dog—and he'll bark in the future because it worked to make the scary thing go away. Negative reinforcement often builds on the pet's avoidance or escape response. It may take only one or two experiences for Sheba or Rex to "learn" this response.
- INTERMITTENT REINFORCEMENT means the positive treat, or negative mailman's departure doesn't happen every time, only intermittently. This teaches the pet that since it happens sometimes, it's worth a try. Intermittent reinforcement increases the likelihood of repetition of the good or bad behavior.

TRAINING STYLES

The old-style coercion methods popularized after World War II that often relied on positive punishment are less popular today. "Physical training" style uses pushing or pulling the pet into position with your hands on his rump to force a sit.

"Punishment" training teaches pets to dislike training and the owner. Yes, pets often obey out of fear of reprisals, but the method also teaches "avoidance" behaviors. Slapping or shaming the kitten for going potty in the house teaches her either to hide it better, or only poop when you aren't around. Punishment training in shy and aggressive pets makes these behaviors worse.

These techniques rely on dominating the pet. For example, the old style of training said you should "correct" a pet for showing aggression. But today behaviorists understand that aggression is caused by stress/anxiety, and punishing the cat increases the stress rather than diminishing it. Punishment causes aggression to escalate.

A NEW WAY TO TRAIN

Modern trainers focus more on "say please" type programs that encourage cats to offer behaviors in order to get all good things in life. The leader of the social group controls the good stuff, such as food and toys. That means owners automatically give themselves a high-ranking status without having to intimidate or use force in any way. Modern training improves communication between you and your cat and teaches her to want to comply.

"Reward Training" means you allow your cat to discover the behavior you want her to do, and then reward it. She may perform many "bad" behaviors (jumping up, clawing the furniture, grabbing your ankles) until finally she happens to "sit" and is rewarded.

A cat figures out the desired behavior from your body language, verbal praise and the treat, and learns she only gets the reward when she does what you want. The more "wrong" behaviors she performs, the more she learns what WON'T work. This technique trains without giving commands or physical direction—no touching allowed—and works especially well with cats that dislike being moved into position.

CLICKER TRAINING: One of the most popular modern training methods employs clickers (as a secondary reinforcer) to communicate with the pet. The technique teaches pets to recognize the "click" as a signal you wanted her to do THAT (click!) behavior, such as meow or wave a paw. A food reward linked to the click reinforces the message. This painless way to train puts no pressure on you or the pet, because you've not "told" her to do anything, so she's never wrong. But she's only "right" when she figures out the correct behavior. Clicker training encourages cats to think and figure out what pleases you to turn owners into a treat machine.

LURE TRAINING: Luring the cat with a reward is the fastest, easiest, most effective and enjoyable training technique of all. The basic sequence is 1) request 2) response 3) reward. This training method teaches cats not only to respond to commands, but also teaches pets to listen and react to humans, and humans to watch and react to the pet. It enhances communication between you as you teach Sheba your language, while you learn her language as well.

EMOTIONAL HEALING

Cats don't have deadlines to meet or a mortgage to pay, but they suffer stress just the same—anything from meeting the new baby or change in your work schedule can leave tails in a twist. You can't always explain that there's nothing to fear, and when pets get emotional they can't learn. Behavior modification and training methods won't work until the pet gets her feelings under control.

TOUCH THERAPY

A specialized massage technique called TTouch developed by Linda Tellington-Jones works particularly well to relieve cat behavior problems, especially aggression and fearfulness. Tests show that TTouch changes the electrical activity in pets' brains. This helps them relax so they're open to learn new ways to cope, rather than just react out of fear.

TTouch uses very specific circular stroke patterns on the surface of the skin all over the pet's body, with extra attention to the ears. The basic circle technique is called the "Clouded Leopard TTouch," because the strokes follow the circle shape of leopard spots.

Make the circles with one or two fingers depending on the size of your cat. Push the skin in a clockwise direction by "drawing" a complete circle with your fingers. Completing the circle changes the brain waves (this has actually been measured!). After completing each circle, slide your hand on the pet's body an inch or two, and form another circle—never lose contact with the body. Continue making "chains" of circles all over, as long as the cat allows.

A ten to twenty minute session is a good target. Let your cat tell you if she wants a light touch or stronger pressure.

Body wraps can also have a positive effect. While most cats object to being hugged which can make them feel trapped, there are specific techniques that produce the opposite emotion. TTouch wraps effectively uses touch to soothe pet emotions. The wraps use lengths of gauze or bandages wrapped in a specific technique around the body and legs to create snug, constant pressure that also helps relieve stress. A properly fitted halter may have a similar effect.

Your cat may also benefit from Thundershirt which has become available for cats. Originally created to relieve anxious behaviors of dogs stimulated by thunder or other noise phobias, the close-fitting vest works on the same principle as TTouch wrap technique. The Thundershirt comes sized for small, medium and large cats and can reduce excess vocalization and other behaviors associated with stress of vet visits or introductions to other pets.

BACH FLOWER REMEDIES

Flower essence therapy can also help with behavior modification. These herbal remedies are made from plants, trees and bushes. The essences are said to carry the imprint of the plant's energy, so the patient's body somehow "recognizes" this image, which wakes up the system so it can heal itself. In a percentage of cases, flower essence therapies work extraordinarily well.

The most familiar products are Bach Flowers composed of 38 individual remedies. Each benefits a different emotional state, and is sometimes used in combination with others for greater effect. Rescue Remedy, for instance, is a premixed combination of the essences Impatiens, Star of Bethlehem, Cherry Plum, Rock Rose and Clematis, recommended for any kind of stress. Most health food stores carry Bach Flower remedies. They're safe to use alongside other medical treatments, and choosing the "wrong" essence won't cause harm. Once you've chosen your flower essences, here's how to put them to work.

- Maintain the original undiluted bottle as your stock bottle. It should last a very long time.
- To create a treatment strength mixture, place two drops of the undiluted remedy in a one-ounce glass dropper bottle, and then fill the bottle three-quarters full with spring water, and shake 100 times. Don't use tap water or distilled water—they go stale too quickly. Refrigerate the mixture. It lasts up to two weeks.
- Give the pet four drops four times a day from the treatment bottle until the behavior changes. This could be anywhere from a few days to a couple weeks. It can be given straight from the treatment bottle dropper into the pet's mouth or on his nose if this doesn't stress him out too much. Don't touch the dropper to the pet or that could contaminate the bottle.
- Alternatively, add drops to a treat, like a teaspoonful of plain yogurt, or add several drops of the remedy to the drinking water for all the pets to sip.

PHEROMONE THERAPY

Pheromones are chemical signals that communicate directly with the brain via the nose on an almost instinctive level, and can be used to "talk" to your cats and put them in a better state of mind to accept learning and training. Dr. Patrick Pageat created Feliway, an analogue of the F3 fraction of the feline cheek pheromone, which cats use to identify/mark their physical environment.

Basically, the substance tells the kitty brain, "Your environment is familiar and safe, so chill, calm down, everything's cool." Feliway comes as a plug-in product for indoors, or as a spray, and is available at most pet products stores. You can use the spray by treating a cloth or bed and placing it inside the cat carrier during travel, or use the plug-in to affect all the cats in a house during introductions.

The plug-in lasts for about four weeks, and works well in enclosed rooms (500-650 square feet). It is particularly helpful for dealing with stress-related marking behaviors such as scratching and urine spraying, and eases the stress toward or fear of other felines or a new environment. It takes 24-48 hours for the plug-in to reach ideal heating rate to spill the pheromone into the air, and about one to two weeks before you'll see a difference in behavior.

Sergeant's Pet Care Products offers a pheromone collar for cats that reproduces the calming pheromones nursing mothers release to soothe kittens. For cats that tolerate collars well, this can be an excellent option.

Other companies offer products that use herbal combinations or essential oils said to simulate the effects of appeasing pheromones. While pheromone therapy has great benefits for many cats, it is not a magic wand. These products work best when used alongside behavior modification and/or other therapies.

TEACHING THE BASICS

Ideally, every kitten learns the rules of the house just as every child learns basic manners. Before anything else, agree with the rest of your family what rules apply. If pets know one human allows sofa digging but not the other, they'll capitalize on that information.

It's helpful for multiple pets to not only know their individual name but also respond to a "group name" such as "kitties." Teach all the critters to pay attention by saying the word-command, then treating every pet that looks at you. Make a huge deal over praising and giving special treats only to those pets that respond and come when called, for example. Before long, all of the "critters" will compete with each other to see who gets the treat first—they won't want to be left out. This also saves time so you can call all the cats to an inside room at once in case of weather emergency, for example.

One of the keys to training involves breaking behaviors down into manageable components, and working backwards to train one thing at a time until you've "chained" all the components together. Trying too much all at once frustrates you and the pet. Pets chain their own behaviors naturally, repeating the same routines each day on the same schedule. Sheba wakes you at 6:30 a.m., follows you to the bathroom, leaps onto the sink, sits, then sips water from the faucet while you shower. Pay attention to the natural behaviors the cat already performs, pick the ones you like, and reward for doing them—and voila! You've trick-trained Sheba to sit on command, for example. It helps in multi-pet homes to have one command (sit or down) your cats reliably perform.

Many very short training sessions (even 5 to 15 seconds) work better than fewer marathon sessions that wear you both out. Concentrate on one behavior in each session, to keep from confusing your pet. Repetition is very helpful and important in first trainings. Both you and your pets need the incentive and inspiration of ending with success, so if he doesn't "get it" build his confidence by asking for a behavior/trick he already knows— and reward him lavishly to end the session.

Give up on the idea of democracy or equality within your pets. Cats don't expect life to be fair all the time and they need to learn how to cope with disappointments without throwing tantrums and being pushy or rude to get their way. Never reward rude behavior or you'll create a furry monster that rules the household. Instead teach your cats that the only way they get access to treats, toys and attention is with polite, patient behavior. You'll all enjoy each other more.

Teaching "Sit"

Train one pet at a time. Situate other cats to watch from behind a baby gate so they get a preview and also learn by observation. Make the game unbelievably fun with a high-value reward for the first pet you work with, so the others can't wait until their turn to train.

1. Say "sit."
2. Lure the cat to sit, using her preferred reinforcer (treat, feather). Lift the treat upwards in front of her nose, so she must lift her head up to watch. As her nose follows the treat, to keep her balance, her butt must hit the ground.
3. As soon as she sits,
4. Reward with the treat or toy.
5. Repeat 1-4, many times a day, every day. Within a short time, your pet will figure out she gets the treat even quicker if she simply plants her tail as soon as you say "sit" and you'll not have to bother luring any longer.
6. Once Sheba understands and knows how to "sit" on command, it becomes the ticket to good things. To get fed or receive attention they must first "pay" with a sit.

Leash Training Cats

A leash works great as a management tool when dealing with a multicat household. The leashed cat's movements can be controlled to interrupt aggressive interactions, for example. Training also builds confidence in shy cats which can help with picked on pariah kitties.

A cat wearing a leash can safely explore worlds outside the confines of the house. Cat leash training especially helps former strays or outdoor felines being transitioned to an exclusively indoor lifestyle. A walk around the garden can relieve the stress and serve as a training reward.

A figure-8 harness tightens so your cat can't wriggle out and escape. These often come already attached to a leash. The small H-harnesses made for dogs may also work. A properly fitted harness also can help calm feline stress in a similar benefit that TTouch body wraps or cat Thundershirt offer. Further, if not correctly fitted the cat can escape which rewards her for struggling to get away, and encourages a repeat of this behavior.

A light weight fabric or corded leash won't weigh down the cat. Look for six-foot or shorter lengths to keep the cat nearby. Ranging too far away can cause problems if the cat becomes tangled in furniture or a rosebush, or has a face-off with another critter, so I don't recommend the retractable spooled leashes for that reason.

Cat Leash Training, Step-By-Step

- Make the halter and leash part of the furniture—that is, leave it out for the cats to find, cheek rub, and explore.
- Pet the cats with the halter to make it smell like them.
- If your cats react to catnip, put the halter and leash in a plastic baggy with the herb to marinate overnight so it gives them a pleasant "high" when encountered.
- Drag the leash around like a toy, and praise Kitty when she catches it, to associate the leash with fun times. Make the leash-chase-game part of her routine, always beginning the process with the halter-petting. Do this for at least a week before you ever attempt to put the halter on your cat.
- Once the leash and halter have become part of her normal routine, sit on the floor to play with the cat first and then put

the halter on her. Some cats immediately accept the odd feeling (especially clueless kittens).

- Many cats wearing a halter for the first time fall over and act paralyzed, as if the constraint makes it impossible to move. Use the leash to tempt another chase-and-catch game or tempt the cat to move with a feather lure. Once cats realize the halter doesn't prevent movement, they become willing to explore. Leave the halter on for only five minutes and then remove.
- Each day have the cats wear the halter for brief periods. Slowly increase halter-wearing time. Remember to reward the cats with play or treats to help associate good things with the experience.
- When the cats no longer object to the halter, clip on the leash and hold it while following him around. Allow cats to lead the way—the leash isn't to drag your cats around, but to give them freedom to safely explore and a safety net for you to "rescue" just in case. You can use the feather lure toy to engage the cats' interest in going where you want them to go.

Go To Your Room!

Cats often need to be safely confined, as a part of re-learning bathroom protocol, being transported for veterinary treatment, or to prevent destructive behavior that can result from boredom or panic attacks. Our Texas weather can turn dangerous and require taking shelter, and it can save the cat's life if she responds to your request without having to chase her down. Upset pets can injure themselves when they pull the drapes off walls or claw through window screens to escape.

To protect the pets from themselves and your house from destruction, confine the worst offenders in a small room. One "bad apple" often can cause everyone to indulge in the bad behavior, so separating the problem child from the rest helps keep everyone in check. Other times, you may wish to give the picked on pet a "safe place" where the others can't reach her. It may not bother some pets to spend time alone, but others get more upset by being confined, so introduce the concept gradually. Pets should view necessary confinement as a happy safe place, and not a punishment. Train one or two at a time (if they get along) but allow the others to watch so they'll want in on the fun.

- Play a game and have your pets run in and out of the area three to five times in a row to bat around catnip mice you toss inside. Play this game every evening for several days, without shutting door.
- After they go in without hesitation, shut the door for one second. Open it before they finish eating the treat or playing so they know the door always opens and won't trap them inside.
- After several sessions, instead of a treat, toss in a puzzle toy stuffed with Philly cream cheese or other tasty treats. Shut the door while they snack. Pets should only get this bonanza treat when in the room with the door shut.
- After week or so, leave Sheba for longer periods with puzzle treats. Once they really enjoy the game, walk away for 30 seconds. Come back before they finish so you can open door and take the toy away. That way they learn they ONLY gets the toy/treat when you aren't there, and learn that good things happen only when you leave and the door shuts.
- Continue to extend time alone from 30 seconds, to a minute, and so on. Once you reach five minutes, you can jump to 30 minutes pretty easily. From there, extending time to an hour and then two hours goes pretty quickly. Use the same area or different ones for your various cats, whatever works best. If pets are happier confined together, do so—just provide enough treat/toys for everyone so there's no squabbling.

Crate Expectations

All cats need to travel at some point, if only to and from the veterinarian, and crate training simplifies the process. There's nothing more dangerous than a loose cat in the car—unless it's more than one! They can get under your brake pedal, distract the driver, and in the worst situation, become furry projectiles if you have an accident. Besides moving, crates can also be used to retrain and/or segregate cats if they aggress toward each other, or to provide safe havens for scared pets.

Crates and carriers come in different sizes and up to two small adult pets or three kittens that get along may be able to share facilities. Larger pets and those with "prickly" personalities do best with individual accommodations. You can find soft-sided zipper bags, hard carriers, and suitcase-like travelers with rollers. Cat show enthusiasts stack carriers on wheeled "trollies" and tow multiple pets from cars to the show and back.

Train your cats to ride happily in a crate or carrier by making it appealing. Cats are especially reluctant to accept change so go slowly and begin training at least four to six weeks before you must move them. You can train multiple pets at a time as long as you have enough crates to go around—otherwise, teach the lessons one on one. Once one claims the first carrier, the rest may become anxious to get in on the fun.

- Rub the carrier inside with catnip or toss in a catnip toy to encourage feline exploration.
- Spray a bit of Feliway on a blanket or towel, and leave inside the carrier for a kitty bed.
- Toss in a Ping Pong ball to create a kitty playground. Play games with your cat and the crate every evening for a week, without shutting the door.
- Make the crate a part of the furniture, rather than a scary and strange object that only appears to herald a vet visit. Take the door off or unzip the opening, and set the carrier on the floor in the living room.
- Leave tasty treats inside for the cat to find, to turn the crate into a treat dispenser.
- After Sheba goes in without hesitation, shut the door for one second, then open as the pet finishes eating the treat. That tells her the door always opens and won't trap her inside.
- After several sessions, instead of a treat, toss in a puzzle toy stuffed with tuna, Philly cream cheese or a catnip toy. Shut the door while the pet snacks. Make sure cats only get this special bonanza treat when in the carrier with the door shut.
- After a week where Sheba begins to enjoy the treat/crate sessions, start increasing the time spent inside. Carry the crate around the house before opening the door for her to come out.
- Try stuffing the kitty puzzle toy with goodies, and tie it inside the crate, then close the door with the pet outside. Wait until the cat begs to get in, and then open the door. The pet must choose either to chew the treat inside the crate, or not at all. Most cats quickly learn that the crate is fun.
- Eventually, carry the crated cat into the car, and take short rides before returning home and letting her out. Each pet will have a different learning curve—some do better if they see outside, while others remain calmer if a cover shields the view.

PART TWO

COMMON PROBLEMS AND PRACTICAL SOLUTIONS

Chapter 4
CAT-EGORICAL AGGRESSION

In multi-cat homes, cats usually aggress toward other cats and rarely toward owners. Signs include outright attacks to urine spraying, or staring at another cat until he moves. Adult cats normally aggress toward strange animals that trespass on their territory, which makes new cat introductions a challenge for owners. There are several categories of feline aggression, and more than one can happen concurrently. The more kinds the cat expresses, the poorer becomes the prognosis for improvement.

Cats bluff incredibly well and fur rarely flies. Dominance displays can be so subtle that you may never know any controversy took place. Almost all types have a fear or anxiety component. This holds true especially during pet introductions or in multiple cat households where dynamics often shift with age, health status, and stress levels.

Oftentimes, people accidentally teach aggression when they reward bad behavior, by allowing the cat to get her way. For instance, if they cut short the grooming when the cat hisses, Sheba subsequently "generalizes" the lesson and uses a hiss or bite to control other interactions. Owners who act anxious or threatening in the cat's presence further aggravate feline aggression.

Recognizing potential triggers and understanding the warning signs of aggression will help you to avoid or diffuse aggression. Common situations during which your cat may react with aggression include:

- When feeling pain
- When a deaf or blind cat is startled
- When approached/disturbed while resting

- When overcrowded by too many cats for the space
- When protecting resources (bed, territory, kittens)
- When physically and/or verbally disciplined
- When forced to make prolonged eye contact
- When experiencing unwelcome handling (being held, petted, lifted)
- When restrained, or forced into unwelcome positions
- When hearing certain music frequencies or high pitched sounds (i.e., baby crying, violin playing)

WHEN THE FUR FLIES: CALCULATING RISK

Most cats learn early on how to wrangle without physically hurting each other. Kitties have exquisite control of their teeth and claws, and know how to pull punches to keep damage to a minimum. They posture, show teeth and swipe claws near (but not in contact with) the target, rather than biting. This allows them to resolve differences without hurting each other.

Thunder and fury with no blood spilled indicates they have excellent bite inhibition but few fights resulting in lots of damage indicate that at least one of the cats either has very poor inhibitions, or seriously wants to kill the other cat. Cats that hate each other and draw blood during fights have an extremely poor prognosis.

Kittens develop good manners through interaction with other kittens and Mom-cat's discipline. Too often, though, kittens go to new homes before they've learned these important lessons and you'll need to teach them.

COMFORT ZONE: BOTTLED FRIENDSHIP

Dr. Patrick Pageat, a researcher in the field of pheromones, discovered five "fractions" of the feline cheek pheromone. Three of these fractions have been identified: F2 communicates information about sexual behavior, and the F3 fraction marks the physical environment and has been marketed as the product Feliway.

"The F4 is a collection of specific molecules common to all cats, that says friend," says Dr. Daniel Mills, a researcher conducting trials on new pheromone products. "It's used to identify friend from foe, so they don't shoot down their own plane," he says. Dr. Pageat has created an analogue of the F4 fraction, marketed as Felifriend, useful in countering cat-on-cat aggression and soothing new cat introductions. The product communicates to all the cats that they already know the individual, have a good relationship, and don't need to fight.

"A problem has been that F4 smells like a very old cheese," says Dr. Pageat. "Even for a French guy, a very strong odor. Our first product was not so comfortable for humans." The new version of Felifriend is available overseas.

In the United States, the product Feliway MultiCat formula addresses cat-to-cat tensions using the feline appeasing pheromone mother cats produce while nursing to comfort kittens. The calming effect works on cats of all ages and helps enormously with cat-on-cat aggression.

TEACHING LIMITS

Cats use mouths and paws to explore their world. You can't stop it, nor should you try. Bite inhibition teaches Kitty to inhibit the force of the bite, and keep claws unfurled, by explaining to her in terms she understands that teeth and claws hurt. She can still make an emphatic point bopping another cat (or human) with a soft paw. Begin training as soon as you get your kitten or cat. A well-socialized adult cat teaches the best lessons to kittens, but you can help, with these tips.

- Allowing cats to play with your hands, fingers or toes encourages biting and may backfire.
- Instead offer a legal toy for the cat to bite and bunny kick.
- Gently praise Sheba for soft paws (claws withheld) or a soft mouth, saying, "Good paws, good mouth!"
- HISS! if the claws come out or the mouthing hurts, just as another cat or kitten would to stop the games.

- If she bites and won't let go, push your hand/arm IN toward the bite to prompt Sheba to release you. Pulling away from the bite stimulates her to bite even more.
- Treat your clothing as an extension of skin and make it off limits, or the kitten won't learn the difference between clawing jeans and nailing your bare legs.
- If the cat or kitten bites or claws during play, and doesn't react to a HISS, instead use a very short, loud, high-pitched EEEK! Warn the rest of your family before doing this, though, so they won't call for help.
- Physical punishment only makes cats more determined to fight back and protect themselves, but they often understand the emotion of hurt feelings. Tell Sheba, "You hurt me," with as much angst and tears as you can muster.
- Very friendly cats understand a "time out." If Sheba can't contain her teeth and claws, send her into a room alone for five minutes to tell her she's exceeded the proper bounds.

VET ALERT!
THYROID DISEASE

Changes in a cat's thyroid hormone production can prompt changes in behavior, especially aggression. Dr. Beaver characterizes hyperthyroid aggression as "nasty" and hypothyroid aggressive cats as "grumpy." A routine blood test screening for thyroid function, especially in middle aged to older cats, diagnoses this treatable condition.

COMBAT INTERVENTION

Screaming felines facing off for battle keeps the faint of heart—and savvy owners—a safe distance away. In fact, you likely will get bitten by physically interceding. Patricia McConnell, Ph.D, a certified applied animal behaviorist, also warns against shouting or yelling. "That can escalate the arousal and make it worse," she says. Most caterwauling is for show, though, and can be headed off before the teeth and claws engage.

- Interrupt the hissing with a favorite toy, such as a fishing pole lure or flashlight beam. Don't wait until the cats fight. The earlier you intervene, the quicker the cats will chill. Choose toys that keep you a safe distance away.
- A loud noise like an air horn or hiss of aerosol spray may work to startle the combatants apart.
- When noise doesn't stop them, soaking with water usually halts the fight. It doesn't take much. Toss half a glass of ice-cold water at them, aiming for their bodies and avoiding the face and eyes.
- If the fight happens in the house and you can't throw water, just toss a thick blanket over top of both cats. That usually separates the pair.
- Wrap up the aggressor cat in the blanket to protect yourself, and bundle her into a room alone for a time out. It takes cats 24 to 48 hours to settle down after arousal. Just the sight of each other can start the fight all over again.
- Catfights may trigger other cats to join in, or fight among themselves. If you have more than a pair, be sure all the cats seem calm. If not, separate each cat into a different room or crate until all have settled.

CAT BASHING

Any two cats can develop a dislike for each other, but most intercat aggression involves intact same-gender cats and worsens during mating season. Neutering before 12 months decreases or prevents up to 90 percent of cat-on-cat aggression. Cats typically work out their place in the hierarchy through posturing without injury to either party. The lowest ranking cat may be targeted, and picked on by the other felines. Acting like a victim can bring out the bully in the dominant feline and prompt additional aggression. Never allow cats to "fight it out" as that rarely settles conflicts but makes matters worse.

Cat-on-cat fights can result from any other kind of aggression. Increased conflicts arise due to changes in the social group as people or animals become part of the household or leave the family group. Major changes to environment, such as moving, or subtle changes such as where cats sleep, eat, perch, and eliminate can cause the fur to fly. Cats reach social maturity at two to four years of age when many cats first challenge others for status.

Not enough space predisposes cats to territorial disputes. Cats mark property with cheek rubs, patrolling, and urine marking. Some diabolical felines lure others into their territory and then "discipline" the other cat for trespassing. Feline territorial aggression is notoriously hard to correct, and marking behavior is a hallmark of potential aggression. Outdoor cats are more aggressive on their home turf and the cat closest to home usually wins the dispute. When all tactics have failed to stop two indoor cats from fighting, then ultimately one cat may need to be placed in a new home or permanently segregated from the other in another part of the house.

When trying to establish authority, cats employ a variety of signals to elevate their status in the eyes of the other felines. They challenge each other with stares, forward-facing body position, hisses and growls, mounting behavior and nape bites, or blocking access to food, play, or attention. Some dominant cats use "power grooming" behavior—energetically licking the other cat—to make her move away. Often, older or weaker cats are victimized and picked on by healthier felines. Manage with behavior modification, counter-conditioning, and sometimes drug therapy. The tips below can help ease the strain and in some instances resolve intercat aggression.

- Increase the territorial space to reduce the urge to wrangle by providing sufficient climbing, hiding, and perching areas.
- Electronic cat doors that can only be opened by the collared victim cat will allow her to access the entire home yet retreat to a safe area the aggressor can't follow. These pet doors open in response to the magnetic "key" inside the collar, or microchip. Look for "keyed" pet doors at pet products stores or on the Internet.
- Don't reward undesirable behavior by offering the aggressive cat food or attention to calm down. If you can catch Sheba before she gets hissy, you can redirect her behavior with an interactive toy, such as a flashlight beam, to lure her into play in another direction. That can also help her associate good things with the other cat.
- If the toy doesn't work, interrupt with an aerosol hiss, and then reinforce the desirable response—acting calm—by offering a treat, toy or attention.
- As long as the cats act aggressively toward each other, treat them as though introducing the cats for the first time. However, with

reintroductions it's best to give the victim cat the choice location of the house, and sequester the bully cat in the isolation room.

- If you see no significant improvement within a week, talk with your veterinary behaviorist to see if drug therapy may be helpful. Drugs may help control the aggressive behavior and decrease the defensive posturing and vocalizing of the threatened cat. You'll still need to provide the cats with a desensitization and counter-conditioning program, but drugs may help training work more effectively.

- Once the signs of aggression, anxiety, and/or hyper-vigilance fade, desensitization and counter conditioning can begin. Gradually expose the cats to each other in very controlled situations. Begin with the cats in carriers, or controlled with a harness and leash, at opposite ends of your largest room or longest hallway.

- During each session feed cats tasty foods or engage in play. This helps both cats learn to associate each other with fun, positive rewards.

- Interrupt unacceptable behavior by the aggressor cat with a hiss of compressed air. Toss small treats to reinforce "good" behavior. Counter conditioning can take months and require much patience and time.

- Once cats have learned to tolerate each other and are allowed to freely roam, create at least two feeding stations and two bathroom locations. Locate them so cats won't be trapped or surprised when using either.

SCAREDY CATS

Fear is the most common reason for feline aggression. Influenced by heredity and shyness, some cats aggress every time they become frightened. Punishment and poor socialization can also cause fear aggression, and will make it worse. Cats may develop fear of people, places, other cats, certain noises, or even odors, and react with aggression, making it difficult for them to enjoy their lives and hard for you to enjoy their company.

Cats often learn to associate one scary experience—car ride to the vet— with all future car rides. A single "bad" episode with a longtime feline friend can turn the relationship sour. Scared cats quickly learn that aggressive behavior makes the scary "thing" go away, and use it repeatedly to warn off strangers, for example.

Affected cats may turn from offense to defense and back again during the arousal. They display a mix of defensive body signals (ears flattened sideways, tail tucked, crouching, and leaning away) and aggressive signals (fluffed fur, showing teeth, hissing, growling, swatting, biting, and scratching). Usually the pupils of their eyes dilate wide, unrelated to the amount of light present. If the cat's aggression is mild and you can keep Sheba away from triggers, no other treatment may be necessary. These tips can help.

- Identify the reactive distance at which the scared cat becomes agitated if another cat approaches. Avoid situations by maintaining appropriate distance between the fearful cat and potential triggers.
- Provide additional quiet areas and/or hiding places in the home. Elevated perches such as cat trees, shelf space, and small boxes help Sheba feel more secure.
- Separate aggressive cats so they can't see each other. Visual contact heightens cat arousal and can increase aggressive episodes or make them worse.
- Use Feliway, in a plug-in or spray form, which is available at pet products stores.
- Create a house of plenty by providing lots of toys, scratching posts, and litter boxes (at least one per cat, plus one) to reduce competition with other cats.
- Use interactive play to build feline confidence. A fishing pole toy or the beam of a light pointer allows the cat to have fun with you, but from a distance not likely to trigger an attack.
- Training cats to do tricks builds confidence and helps improve the bond you share. For more details, refer to the training section.
- Rescue Remedy can help shy and fearful pets, so add several drops to their water.
- Fearful cats often learn to turn aggression "on" immediately at the sight of another cat with which they've argued. Behavior modification using counter conditioning teaches Sheba to tolerate the other feline. To begin the program, each cat should be segregated in her own room.
- Then create a 15-minute routine and repeat three to four times every single day with each cat in private. This could include the cat's meal, a special playtime, grooming session, or other pastime Sheba enjoys, to reduce fear of the unexpected.

- Measure a bit beyond the cats' reactive distance in a single room or long hallway. Place two cages/carriers with one at each end, or use a pair of baby gates to keep the cats separated outside of that reactive distance. When using carriers, spray a bit of Feliway on a cloth and leave it inside before inserting the cat.

- Feed each cat lots of treats, talk in a happy, upbeat voice, and scratch their cheek/chins through the crate to make the experience pleasant. Cats willing to take treats while seeing each other are not as fearful. Do this several times a day for three to five minutes at a time before returning them to their private rooms.

- Slowly decrease the distance between the carriers, continuing with the treats, praise, and petting. This teaches the fearful cat to associate the other kitty's presence with good things while she feels protected inside the carrier.

- Once the fearful cat no longer shows arousal within that critical distance, take out the non-fearful cat. Leave scared kitty inside her carrier, while continuing to treat-treat-treat. Take turns bringing one cat out while the other gets treats in the cage. The cats may never become buddies, but over time, they may be able to tolerate each other without resorting to violence.

CALMING SIGNALS: FELINE RESTRAINTS

Fearful cats often bite without thinking, and pin-wheeling paws cause lots of claw damage. When you know a particular situation (i.e., vet visit) prompts an aggressive outburst, contain the cat's claws and teeth to protect yourself and others.

- Mesh cat muzzles are available from veterinarians and pet product suppliers. They cover the face and eyes, contain the teeth and help calm the cat by shutting out the view. Make sure you choose one that fits properly (they come in several sizes), and that allows air to circulate for appropriate breathing. Flat faced cats like Persians can be more difficult to fit, and also often have more trouble with breathing.

- Commercial "cat bags" typically contain the whole body while the head sticks out, and can keep claws at bay particularly when something on the cat's head needs attention. A pillowcase can work well in a pinch.

IT FEELS TOO GOOD

Owners of multiple cats often experience "petting aggression," also referred to as status-related aggression, especially when these cats don't have the "clout" to boss other felines around but want to control their world. Cats avoid the behavior with those who resist but get pushy with people who give in to demands. They often ask for petting especially when you're cuddling another cat, but then bite you to stop the interaction. That may in part be due to location of the strokes, since cats accept grooming from other cats on the head and neck and may prefer this to body contact.

Physical correction makes the behavior worse. Petting aggression can be explosive and dangerous, and is typical of young energetic cats taken early from their litter, and left alone for long periods during the day. The following tips also can help.

- Identify and avoid situations that might lead to aggression. Use a treat or toy to bribe cats off furniture or out of the way, rather than physically moving them.
- Say, "move" and toss the treat on the floor or entice the cat down with a feather. Eventually, just say the word "move" and offer a sweeping gesture for the cat to obey—and, you've avoided an encounter that could otherwise cause a bite.
- Stand up to dump the cat off your lap before she bites. When you're petting other cats, ignore her when she solicits attention, unless she behaves.
- Limit petting to the cat's head or back of the neck, and identify the cat's petting threshold. Count the number of strokes Sheba enjoys before her ears flatten, tail becomes active, and eyes dilate, and in future stop before you reach her limit.

- Desensitize the cat. If she tolerates three strokes before ears go back, add one more stroke and then stop, and dump her off your lap before she can bite. Add one stroke each week to gradually increase her petting threshold.

ALL WOUND UP

Both predatory and play aggressions include components of stealth, silence, alert posture, hunting postures, and lunging or springing at "prey" that moves suddenly after being still. Nearly any type of movement, from walking to picking up an object, triggers the behavior. Predation directed toward an infant, or smaller pets represents the greatest danger, but over-the-top play is normal and hand raised kittens and those weaned early seem to have increased risk.

They'll terrorize shy cats, bully smaller kittens, and pester geriatric felines as well as targeting owners. Confident adult cats usually put these obnoxious felines in their place, young kittens outgrow the behavior, and tips found in "Teaching Limits" help a great deal. In addition, the following will help you deal with very playful or predatory aggressive cats.

- Provide safe areas where the picked on felines won't be molested, such as high perches or separate rooms.
- Place a bell on the attack cat to warn victims in time to escape, and so you can interrupt and stop the behavior.
- Hissing from an aerosol, a water gun, citronella sprays and other interruptions may stop the attack cold. Experiment to find what works best for Sheba.
- A leash and harness can be attached to the cat for control and interruption of undesirable behavior.
- Play interactive games with all your cats to burn off energy. Move toys perpendicular to line of sight—across cats' field of vision rather than toward or away from her—to spark the greatest interest. Interactive play encourages confidence in shy cats so they'll kick Sheba's furry tail and teach her manners.
- Create a regular routine that includes specific playtimes, so the cats learn to expect fun interactive times.

- A second kitten of the same age, size and temperament could help by providing a legal target and playmate, as well as teaching bite and claw inhibition.

THE BLAME GAME

Redirected aggression happens as a result of Sheba being unable to respond to a physical or verbal correction, or the thwarting of a desire. This affects adult male cats most often and arises from territorial, fear-induced, inter-male or defensive aggression.

When Tom can't reach the squirrel tap-dancing on the trees out the window, he instead nails the closest available victim. That may be another cat or the owner who wanders by at the wrong time, and such attacks seem unprovoked if you never see the squirrel. Owners often think the cat has gone nuts when Tom attacks out of the blue or when cats who previously got along become hostile to each other.

Common triggers include the sight, sound, or odor of another cat, other animals, unusual noise, unfamiliar people or environment, and pain. While people only become the accidental victim in the presence of the trigger, a housemate cat can become a permanent scapegoat after just one "accidental" response. After a first episode, the aggressing cat "remembers" and launches attack whenever he sees the scapegoat cat. The poor scapegoat anticipates attacks, and acting like a victim stimulates the aggressor to continue the behavior. Refer to the section on "Cat Bashing" to help stop the cat aggressor/victim pattern. The following suggestions also help prevent future cases of redirected aggression.

- Leave the cat alone when you know he's aroused and you notice chittering teeth and active tail. Try to keep the other cats from bothering him as well, especially when he lounges in the windowsill.
- Keep stray cats and strange animals away from window sight of your property. (See Shooing Stray Cats Away).
- Prevent access to windows or partly cover them to keep your cats from seeing the triggers. Pull the blinds, and move furniture away from windows. Double-sided tape products such as Sticky Paws (www.stickypaws.com) applied to windowsills makes the surface uncomfortable so cats avoid lounging.

- Separate cats that show aggression toward each other. It may take several days or weeks for the aroused cat to "forget" the association and stop picking on the victim cat. Time away helps the scapegoat stop acting like a victim, too—which helps reduce the chance of being picked on.
- Bell the aggressor cat so the victim kitty can avoid encounters.

Shooing Stray Cats Away

Outdoor roaming cats cause your indoor felines no end of angst. Your cats feel proprietary toward even the yard that they see through windows. They don't even have to see—just smell each other—and the hissing party begins. The presence of a strange cat prompts hit-or-miss litter box behavior, redirected aggression, and stress-related behaviors or health problems for your indoor cats.

While you shouldn't ever be cruel to strays or ferals, your first obligation must be to your own pets. When you know the owner of a neighborhood cat, contact them about the problem. If the cats have no owner, contact the local shelter about capture-and-adoption options. Feral stray cat populations can be helped with resources from Alley Cat Allies (www.alleycat.org). Meanwhile, refer to these tips to relieve your cats' behavior problems caused by outdoor cats.

- Wash Walls. Cats urine-spray to mark territory and the smell draws them back again and again to re-baptize the spot. They know about your indoor cats and seek to assert their ownership, and that smell also drives your indoor cats crazy. Avoid bleach which smells attractive to cats and will increase spraying. Enzyme-based odor neutralizers are the best option.
- Make Targets Unattractive. Aluminum foil wrapped around door bottoms make urine splash back onto the spraying cat and may persuade stray felines to find other targets. The Ssscat shoos with a "hiss" of air when the motion detector is triggered and can be set nearly anywhere. You can also set up motion-detector water sprinklers that shoot streams of water when critters enter range. For the roofs and hoods of cars, place a plastic carpet runner nub-side up to make this warm place uncomfortable.

- Brush Away Brush. Piles of wood, long grass or other habitat invites mice and other prey attractive to stray cats. If you clear away the clutter—and free meal—stray cats hunt elsewhere.
- Foil Digging. Soft garden soil proves irresistible for outdoor cats to use as a toilet. Before you plant, line beds with chicken wire— vegetation grows through the wire but it's off-putting to the digging cat. Add prickly cuttings from holly leaves, rose clippings, pine cones, or other uncomfortable material that helps keep cat paws at bay. Add the peels of citrus fruit (oranges, lemons, grapefruit) for an off-putting odor—cats don't like citrus smells.
- Try Commercial Repellents. Check the reviews, not all work particularly well. The Cat Stop has received some thumbs up comments, and it works with batteries and a motion detector that triggers a loud sound to shoo away strays.

Mirror Angst

Cat eyes have the ability to discern mirror images. Cat face conformation—eyes at the front for binocular vision—lends itself to seeing reflections. But most times, a reflection doesn't also have a strange odor or unique sounds attached so the reflection isn't important or "real" without a signature odor or noises. But other cats develop problem behaviors from misrecognizing their own reflection as a threat or playmate.

Kittens that have less life experience are most likely to react to reflections before they realize they can't reach that "cat behind the glass." Some cats react to the reflections in pictures, oven doors, fireplace screens, or even tile. Mirrors and other reflecting surfaces can be confused with windows.

Cats often attempt to reach the other cat by pawing underneath or at the side of the mirror to "get around" the barrier preventing contact. Cats also do this after watching TV images of birds or other critters, mistaking the screen for a window.

The lurking outdoor cat presence primes the mirror-gazing kitty to become suspicious so his fearful reflection also triggers defensive body language. When the cat displays "friendly" body language, the reflection does the same and such interactions are less likely to cause problems. But a fearful or aggressive body posture is reflected back to the cat and perceived as a threat, raising the actual cat's arousal. This becomes a vicious cycle.

When cats are highly aroused they react rather than think, and it matters little that the reflection offers no scent or sound. Some cats learn to associate shiny surfaces/locations with feeling upset and these can trigger acting out behavior.

The interaction with the reflection runs the range from curious and playful, to head-thumping and screaming attacks. This could also feed into cases of redirected aggression. In other words, the cat becomes hissed off by that "threatening cat" seen in the mirror, but can't reach the interloper, and so instead nails a passing cat friend.

Each time a cat sees an upsetting reflection he practices being upset. Each repeat of a given behavior predicts more to come, and makes it more likely for it to continue. Reducing the number of instances lowers the potential for a repeat.

- Remove mirrors if possible.
- Move mirrors or problem reflective surfaces. A new location may not have the same associations.
- Cover reflective surfaces you can't move. Tape paper over cat-level mirrors.
- If outside cats are amping up his reactivity, refer to the section on shooing away stray cats.
- Scatter catnip in the locations to give upset cats a pleasurable feline "high" that counters the angst.
- Pheromone products like Comfort Zone with Feliway may calm upset feelings, too.
- Create positive associations with the mirror locations. Use favorite toys, interactive games or treats so the location comes to mean a benefit for the cat.
- When you have one confident cat that ignores the mirror, play games and offer treats in the mirror-area while the upset cat watches. This can teach the upset cat that another feline has no fear, and can encourage copy-cat calm behavior.

VET ALERT!
HYPERESTHESIA SYNDROME

Aggressive behavior without an identifiable cause is referred to as "idiopathic" aggression, but a relatively rare physical condition could be the culprit. Hyperesthesia syndrome, an excessive sensitivity to touch, refers to several odd behaviors (including aggression) that have no recognizable stimulus.

The syndrome first appears in cats one to four years old and Siamese, Burmese, Himalayans and Abyssinians seem to have the highest incidence. Affected cats indulge in excessive grooming that targets their own tail and lower back, and may ultimately result in self-mutilation when Sheba attacks herself. Inexplicable aggression is the second pattern of behavior. Cats seem friendly, and even beg for attention, then furiously attack when the owner attempts to pet them. The final pattern reported by the veterinary literature is seizure.

Some behaviorists believe stress triggers psychomotor seizures that cause the behaviors. Other researchers believe the syndrome parallels human panic attacks and obsessive/compulsive disorders that occur due to the individual cat's personality in combination with the pressures of her environment, frustrations and stress levels.

If you can identify and avoid stress factors that trigger incidents the syndrome may be eliminated. Some cats can be jarred from the behavior by an unexpected sudden noise like clapping your hands, or slapping a newspaper against a table. Cats may also respond to anti-seizure medication or human anti-anxiety drugs and antidepressants that act on the cat's brain to put on the behavior brakes.

Chapter 5
TOILET TECHNIQUES

Cats have a reputation for being fastidious, clean creatures so we expect kittens to be born knowing about toilet etiquette. Doing what comes naturally often gets Sheba in trouble with owners when neither party understands what the other wants out of the deal.

The dirt in the potted palm offers the perfect place to make a feline deposit, especially if the "legal" toilet isn't up to kitty standards. Spraying urine on the doorframe, or on your purse, makes perfect sense—or actually, scents—especially when other cats are around. To the dominant kitty, urine labels the object as hers, and dampens the territorial ardor of other felines. Shouts or inappropriate punishment increase the cat's stress level and frequently prompt an increase in bathroom indiscretions.

An adult cat without elimination problems uses the litter box on average five times per day. The more cats you have, the greater your chances of bathroom problems. Felines have very specific ideas about who should go where, and which cat owns what litter box. Ages of cats and placement of facilities have a great impact. Strays rescued from the neighborhood or shelter that spent previous years outdoors may not have a clue about using an indoor litter box.

CALMING SIGNALS:
WHO DID THE DIRTY DEED?

In multiple cat households, you must identify the culprit(s) in order to treat the right cat. Confinement may help, or ask your veterinarian about "pilling" each cat in turn with fluorescein dye, suggests Dr. Kersti Seskel, a veterinary behaviorist practicing in Sydney, Australia. Six dye strips placed in a gelatin capsule given orally to the cat causes the urine to fluoresce a bright yellow-green color (under a black light) for 24 hours after ingestion. For inappropriate defecation, add shavings of different colored non-toxic crayons to the food of each cat.

HAIRBALL HORRORS

Barefooted owners discover wads of wet fur—hairballs—decorating the most stainable portions of the carpet during the wee hours of the night. Hairballs challenge all cat owners but multi-cat homes must manage more hair. Cats spend up to 50 percent of awake-time grooming themselves. Friendly cats also groom each other, so the more cats, the greater becomes the problem. Swallowed fur that doesn't pass into the litter box becomes hotdog or cigar-shaped wads when vomited.

An occasional hairball, especially from longhaired cats during shedding season, isn't unusual. But large amounts of swallowed fur can block the digestive tract. Fifty percent of feline constipation is due to hairballs, and when cats suffer painful bowel movements they often "blame" the box, and stop using it. There are inexpensive and effective means to prevent hairballs.

- Regularly comb and brush your cats, to reduce the amount they swallow through grooming themselves and each other.
- Feed a "hairball diet." Commercial formulas include added nondigestible fiber that helps push swallowed hair through the digestive tract and into the litter box.

- Mix a teaspoon of plain bran or Metamucil into canned meals. Some cats enjoy grazing on wheat grass, available in grow kits from pet products stores. Flaxseeds or psyllium husks, available in health food stores, also act as natural laxatives and work well. Add ¼ teaspoon of flaxseeds or psyllium for every meal.
- Digestible fats such as butter cause diarrhea or are absorbed before they move the hairball, but non-medicated petroleum jelly works well. Spread the jelly on Sheba's forepaw for her to lick off.
- Canned pumpkin is very rich in fiber, and many cats like it as a treat. Serve a teaspoonful over the cat's regular food a couple of times a week. Divide the can into teaspoon-size dollops and freeze in an ice cube tray, so you can thaw one serving at a time. Commercial products also help the hairball pass more readily.

VET ALERT!

Cats have been known to suffer hairballs as big as baseballs that require surgery to be removed. Frequent vomiting signals intestinal blockage. Hairballs also can cause diarrhea, loss of appetite, wheezing cough or dry retching, or a bloated abdomen. See your veterinarian immediately if your cat exhibits any one or more of these signs.

COVERING BEHAVIOR

Pet cats get rave reviews on cleanliness because they come preprogrammed to cover waste in the litter box. But one of the top behavior complaints of cat owners involves litter box behavior, including cats that refuse to cover.

Covering waste is not a universal cat behavior, and the opposite may be your cat's normal. Feral cats may cover waste if nearer to home and young kittens. Covering or burying waste reduces the scent signals that might alert predators to the presence of defenseless offspring. Feral cats in managed colonies may be more fastidious, as well, in part because the territory is shared. But typical feral cat behavior shows us that wild felines rarely bury feces. They use it to mark territory and so display it. Feral cats often leave waste on grassy tussocks that elevate and make it even more prominent.

To put this in a pet cat perspective, most household cats do bury the waste probably because it's so close to their eating and sleeping areas. Consider that an outdoor free-ranging cat's territory might encompass more than two miles. Locating your cat's litter box across the house from a feeding station is still virtually in the cat's face.

House cats that choose not to cover waste inside the box or that leave a deposit outside the box may simply be doing what comes naturally. One study followed female pet cats out and about and observed them defecate 58 times—and only twice did the cats try to dig a hole first, or cover it afterwards.

Humans also may have encouraged "clean" covering behavior in our pet cats by selectively choosing (and breeding) the ones that cover up waste. But cats that leave their creativity uncovered for the world to admire are not abnormal—they're just being cats.

Cats that previously dug-and-covered in the litter box which suddenly leave a deposit uncovered should be evaluated to ensure it doesn't point to a potential health problem. When the cat receives a clean bill of health, look for potential behavior causes. For instance, this may be the cat's way of sending a smelly signal to other cats (or even a stray hanging around outside the window) that the territory is owned.

MISSING THE MARK

In multi-cat households, hit-or-miss bathroom behavior can be a real problem as cats wrangle to claim position and territory. Problems are split evenly between spraying (urine marking), and urination/defecation misbehavior. Cats squat to empty their bladder and urinate downward on horizontal surfaces, and urinating outside the litter box constitutes "house soiling." Normal marking behavior (spraying) consists of backing up to the target to spray urine on a vertical object, and almost never takes place in the litter box.

Cats do NOT target owner belongings to "get back" at some imagined slight. For some cats, problems result from leaving Mom-cat too early before learning proper bathroom manners.

Hand-raised orphan kittens or those adopted younger than eight to ten weeks often must be taught the basics by owners. Transitioning adult outdoor cats to an indoor lifestyle also requires re-training. Many cats develop a routine, and defecate once or twice a day usually at the same time—and urinate two to six times a day. However, it's not unusual for some adult cats to urinate only once every 36 hours or so. You can use this information to monitor and manage your cats' bathroom activities. A sudden loss of litter box allegiance means either the litter box is unacceptable, the cat feels bad, or the other cats make her avoid the bathroom.

More than 1/3rd of cats with elimination problems have an underlying health condition and if Sheba refuses to use the box to urinate (or defecate) but not both, look for a medical problem. Cats are instinctively clean and want privacy, so they "go" elsewhere if the box is dirty or in a high traffic area. When one cat guards the bathroom facilities, the others leave deposits under the potted palm. A bully may dominate access to the litter box by sleeping in or near the pathway that leads to the toilet, or glaring to keep hopefuls at bay.

Punishment won't work. You must first identify and then remove the cause; re-establish good habits; and prevent a return to the scene of the crime.

- Many cats don't want to "go" after another cat. Others demand a separate box for urine and another for feces, and some dominant cats guard the facilities and won't let the others use it. Use the 1+1 rule to solve litter box woes: provide one litter box for each cat, plus one (that's three boxes for two cats, for example).
- Keep the toilet clean by scooping waste and discarding it at least twice a day. The more cats you have, the greater the amount of waste and ensuing smell which offends you and the cats.
- Adding an automatic litter box helps enormously, because the litter ALWAYS stays clean. However, it may take some training to teach cats to use this facility.
- Be sure to empty and clean the entire box at least once a week. Use scalding hot water but no harsh-smelling disinfectants, because the detergent smell can be just as off-putting to the cats.
- Clean soiled areas thoroughly or the scent will draw Sheba (even innocent bystanders!) back to the scene of the crime. Avoid using ammonia-based products, which cats think smells like the ammonia in their own urine. Use an enzymatic odor neutralizer such as

Petastic that literally eats the odor. Anti-Icky-Poo and Zero Odor get raves from behaviorists and pet owners.

- To find hidden urine accidents, invest in a quality "black light" and shine it around after you've turned off lights in the suspect areas. Cat urine glows under the black light.

- If your cats target plastic or rubber-backed bath mats, toss out the mats. The backing hosts various microorganisms designed to keep the carpet stain-resistant, but it smells like urine to cats, and many felines eliminate on these mats because they already smell like a litter box.

- Cats prefer certain kinds of texture, granularity, and coarseness in the litter. Offer a "smorgasbord" of litter substrates for cats to choose their ideal. Offer sand and potting soil mix for cats used to doing their "duty" outside.

- Change the depth of litter (increase or decrease) or remove the plastic liner to make the box more attractive. Cats that scratch to cover their waste may dislike catching their claws in the plastic liner.

- Once you find a litter your cats like, don't mess with success. Cat Attract Litter (www.preciouscat.com) contains a proprietary herbal blend most cats find irresistible that helps litter box allegiance.

- If your cats prefer the linoleum, wood floor, or bathtub, offer an empty litter box, and then gradually add litter.

- Buy a new box. Plastic holds odor and smelly old boxes offend cats even when you've scrubbed them. Cats that "blame" the old box for a scare or discomfort often eagerly embrace a new facility.

- Covered boxes help contain litter when energetic diggers throw sand everywhere, but they hold odors, and your shy cats may fear being trapped inside and avoid using them. Offer different types of toilets—uncovered or covered—to encourage kitty to choose one. Very large cats may not be able to pose in a standard size box without dropping deposits or urinating over the edge. Offer a much bigger container such as a clear plastic storage bin to accommodate these cats.

- A storage bin type container works well for up to three small to medium cats willing to share, so you can reduce the total numbers of boxes.

- Very young, elderly, or ill cats have trouble reaching the box in time. Provide a toilet on each floor of multi-story homes, or at each end of single-story floor plans to give these felines a better opportunity for a pit stop.

- For tiny kittens, or very arthritic older cats, a regular box may be too large for him to climb in and out, so offer a cookie sheet or cut down the sides of the box.

- If you know or suspect one of your cats guards the toilet from the others, be sure to position litter boxes in more than one location. Sheba can't guard them all at once, and that way at least one is available to the rest of the cats at all times.

- Be sure boxes are in a low traffic area, and quiet location such as a closet or storeroom. Laundry rooms where a dryer buzzer frightens the cat in mid-squat, may be less than ideal.

- Sometimes placing the new litter box right on top of the soiled area encourages cats to use the box in that location. Once they again use the box, gradually move it to a more appropriate area a foot or so a day.

- Make the illegal location unattractive so they willingly use the proper toilet. Give the soiled area a different connotation by placing favorite cat toys, food bowls, bed or scratching post on top of the soiled area, once it's been cleaned.

- The longer house soiling goes on, the harder it is to correct. To reestablish good habits, temporarily confine the problem cats to a small area with a litter box whenever they can't be supervised. Usually cats prefer to use a box rather than having to live with the accident. Behaviorists recommend one week's confinement for every month Sheba has been soiling, but that ratio can be decreased if the problem has been in existence more than six months.

VET ALERT!

"Sixty-five percent of cats with blood in their urine are diagnosed with idiopathic [unknown origin] cystitis," says Dr. Elsey. According to research at Ohio State, although their urine looks normal, the bladder lining is inflamed. That makes the cat hurt when urinating, so she blames the box and goes elsewhere. "We can't routinely detect the inflammation," he says, "so owners just think they have a bad cat." The drug amitriptyline won't cure but can help cats feel better by reducing their stress levels. "Switch from dry to canned food," suggests Dr. Elsey. That doubles the amount of water intake and helps dilute urine to help ease the condition.

TARGET PRACTICE

Urine spraying almost always involves problems between cats. While only about 25 percent of households with a single cat deal with this, every household with ten or more cats suffer this problem. The more cats you have, the greater the likelihood of tiffs resulting in one or more cats "baptizing" your belongings.

Common targets include vertical objects such as windows, computer equipment, curtains, and sliding glass doors. Horizontal targets often include clothes, beds, backpacks, briefcases, and plastic bags. Spraying arises out of anxiety. You must figure out why the cat sprays before you can fix the problem, so determine the social significance of the target's location.

Draw a map or videotape the cat-to-cat interactions to find clues. Perhaps a cat dominates territory with stares and posturing, strays trespass in the yard, or you spend extra time at the computer.

If you can't pinpoint the reason, try many things all at once to manage the environment. After the spraying stops, you can try reducing these options one by one to find the least amount that works.

- Neutering eliminates spraying behavior in 90 percent of the boys; spaying eliminates the behavior in 95 percent of the girls. Get your cats fixed!
- Create a "house of plenty" with lots of food, toys, and territory available so less squabbling occurs.
- Small apartments or homes with many cats must increase the vertical space in the environment. Adding cat trees, bookcases, window perches, and other second-story real estate reduces anxiety between cats so they stop spraying.
- Create a routine. Cats thrive on the status quo, and anything unexpected sends stress levels soaring, potentially increasing the urge to spray.

- Clean illegal targets with an odor neutralizer to help prevent the cat from refreshing the scent again and again. Use odor neutralizers — "Anti-Icky-Poo" (www.antiickypoo.com) created by chemist for pet odor problems, is highly recommended by behaviorists.

- The pheromone product, Feliway, helps calm stress related to the environment, and cats tend not to urine-spray on top of the Feliway cheek scent. The product comes as either a spray, or a plug-in diffuser. It works best when used every single day for up to 30 days. After you've cleaned the illegal targets, spray them with the Feliway and use the plug-in in the room where the cat most often sprays.

- If your cat sprays consistently in only one or two places, make the targets unattractive by covering them with aluminum foil. When the urine hits, the sound startles the cat and stops her in her tracts. It also tends to splash urine back onto the kitty and she'll not like that. The foil lining also makes cleanup easier.

- When you see the cat preparing to spray—backing up with tail erect—interrupt the behavior. Don't yell. Ideally, the interruption should come out of the blue with the cat unaware it came from you. Toss a beanbag, Ping Pong or other toy near the cat (don't hit her) to startle and stop the pose.

- Redirect the behavior. When you see the cat sniffing a danger zone, engage her with a favorite toy. Place toys, a scratching post, or a food bowl in the area to give it a different association instead of the "potty" place.

- When you can't be there, the Ssscat® aerosol (www.ssscat.com) may keep cats away from high-risk targets. It sprays a hiss of air when the cat triggers the built-in motion detector.

VET ALERT!
ANTI-ANXIETY DRUGS

Not all cats respond to environmental management, and this can be a challenge to owners who love their cats but hate living with urine. When spraying arises due to fearfulness, stress, and/or anxiety, veterinary behaviorists recommend you discuss drug therapy options with your veterinarian.

- Two studies have reported that 80 percent of treated cats improved using clomipramine (Clomicalm ®). However, there are serious side effects to consider including potential toxicities.
- An equally effective drug called fluoxetine (Prozac ®) works well with less serious side effects, but spraying behavior returns if the cat goes off the drug. Behavioral and environmental management must continue, along with any drug therapy. Some cats respond as early as the first or second week of treatment, while others require three weeks or more to see results.

CALMING SIGNALS:
PET DOOR TRAINING

When you have a safe outside enclosure for your cat to play and potty, installing a cat flap in a window or patio door allows your cats to come and go rather than you becoming the doorman. Cats naturally rub against objects to leave behind their scent. Use this natural inclination to teach Sheba to push through the cat flap.

Prop the door flap open so the cats can see through to the other side. Use a favorite treat or toy to repeatedly lure her back and forth through the opening until she becomes used to the idea. Next, leave the flap closed, but find an alluring scent that cats can't resist. Catnip, peppermint, or tuna juice painted on the pet door may prompt a cheek rub or forehead butt.

Reward even a nose touch to encourage the behavior. When the first cat pushes through, have a favorite treat waiting and reward her while the others watch. Once they understand that there MAY be a treat waiting, they'll be more inclined to use the cat door (and the bathroom facilities or play opportunities) whether a treat awaits or not.

Note: it's best for cat flaps to be translucent so Sheba can see through and not be ambushed by another cat. There also are cat doors available that "key" open only to the specific cat wearing a corresponding collar or microchip, so you can keep other critters out or limit which cats come and go.

Chapter 6

UPSET KITTY FEELINGS

Cats are just as emotional as people and behavior changes mirror those of owners in similar situations. Stress may be expressed as depression and grief, fearful behavior, insomnia, jealousy or any of a range of emotions. Some cats (Siamese, Burmese, Himalayan and Abyssinians most commonly) relieve stress by over-grooming themselves until they go bald, and once the stress goes away the hair grows back. Physical health problems and instinct can also prompt cats to act out emotionally, so remember to use the P.E.T. Test to figure out the cause.

Pets also react to the emotions their human companions feel. When a cat has bonded deeply with you, she'll react to your emotional state with purrs and snuggles. Changes in the routine almost always upset cats. Changing work schedule, introducing a new cat, or moving to a new home are particularly stressful. One cat feeling out of sorts makes the rest of the felines uneasy, and can cause an emotional meltdown among all the cats. Recognizing your cat's emotional state and understanding why she feels that way allows you to help soothe upset feelings, and ensure the entire feline family stays happy.

FELINE GRIEF

Depression and grief can be worse for cats because we can't explain why a beloved cat or human friend has gone away. Death, divorce, or just leaving for college often leaves one or more of your cats deeply affected, and that always causes a ripple effect that impacts the entire feline household.

For instance, when your top cat becomes depressed, she'll be less patient with the other felines and may lash out with aggression, or if she disappears under the bed, the other cats argue over taking her top position. A new family member (husband, baby) who demands your attention also upsets the cat, because you are the most important part of Sheba's territory. Refer to the section on **Green Eyed Monsters** for tips for dealing with jealousy.

Depressed cats sleep more than usual, avoid company, stop playing, and hide. They don't groom themselves as well, lose their appetite and refuse to eat. Depression affects physical health by compromising the immune system, so pets become more susceptible to disease, and symptoms of depression may mimic other problems. Scratching or urine spraying increases, especially near and on items that you own (your bed, the laundry) because the scent comforts them. For tips on scratching or spraying, see those sections in **Pet Peeves.**

Time heals grief, and cats that have bonded closely with other pets or people can become attached to new loved ones. Supporting the feelings of a grief-stricken cat helps her more quickly return to normal, and interact with the rest of the felines in a healthy manner.

- The death of a pet devastates the whole family, including the other pets. It can help surviving cats to understand by letting them "say goodbye" to the deceased pet's body. Expect any sort of reaction, from sniffing the body, ignoring it, or crying. A last look allows cats to understand the deceased won't return, and prevents the tortured searching some grieving pets display.

- Losing somebody special depresses you, too, and cats act like sponges that soak up your emotion, so talk to her, and be positive. Your cats won't understand the words but will recognize your intent.

- When a human family member leaves on vacation or college, keeping scented items as reminders can help soothe cats until the beloved's return. Seal a few unwashed socks in a baggy, and bring one out now and then for Sheba to sleep or play with as a security blanket. The long-distance human can also mail scented objects home to the cat.

- The scent of the departed pet lingers in the house and can be a frightening reminder to surviving cats that were less dominant. Remove those toys or beds used by the deceased pet, so the remaining felines don't avoid that area.

- Light therapy benefits people suffering from depression by affecting the production of hormones from the pituitary and endocrine glands. Cats are natural sun worshipers and a sunbath for twenty minutes a day can raise kitty spirits. Set up a soft blanket on a table near a sunny window for feline lounging.
- Peppy music can help Sheba beat the doldrums, so try playing the radio or CDs that have a fast, upbeat tempo.
- A specialized massage technique called TTouch reduces your cat's depression. Pay particular attention to her ears, face and neck.
- The Bach Flower remedy Gentian works well for general depression, while Gorse works better for severe depression. Star of Bethlehem commonly is recommended for sorrow and grief. Put four drops into the water bowl for all-day sipping, or add drops to a treat, like a teaspoonful of plain yogurt.

SHRINKING VIOLETS

Some cats grow up to be worrywarts, and acting fearful or shy is like wearing a "kick me" sign that prompts the other cats in your household to pick on them. Up to 20 percent of any population of a given species will be born prone to introversion and fear. Some cats acquire the traits from poor or missing socialization or from a lack of proper nutrition during gestation. Kittens whose mothers received poor nutrition prior to giving birth are more "reactive" than normal and often suffer fearfulness and shyness.

An intensely unpleasant experience can lead to a "memory" of the event, in which cats generalize the fear to similar future events. A onetime abuse situation or single bad experience with another cat or the car makes Sheba fearful of all cats, car rides, or men.

Signs of anxiety include decreased grooming, reduced social interactions, and appetite loss. The fearful cat signals unease by looking away, holding ears down and sideways, shaking, crouching, urinating or defecating. Stress strains the immune systems, and fearful felines are unhappy pets. Some types of fear never go away, but with lots of patience, you can help the cat feel more comfortable in her home.

- Adopting pairs of kittens together, or a mother with a baby, can give the new pets an ally to build confidence and ward off shyness. Some kitties dislike other cats, but don't feel threatened by a dog.

A friendly, gentle dog may be the best confidence builder for a shy cat. Refer to the chapter on cat-dog introductions.

- Identify all the different sights, places, sounds, odors, people or other things that cause fear. You need to know what she fears before you can address those issues.

- During the spring mating season, cats act more fearful because of the noises of stray cats or wild animals they hear outside. A white noise machine can cover up or mute these distressing sounds, or tune your radio to static.

- Anything irregular or unpredictable can cause feline fear, so create a schedule so she can rely on when to expect meals, petting, or chase the feather game.

- When Sheba becomes scared and can't hide, stress levels skyrocket. Give her lots of places to stay out of sight, such as kitty "tents" placed in strategic places, and collapsible cat tunnels that create safe pathways through the center of rooms, especially in open areas where Sheba feels exposed. That can encourage her to move around the house more, and build confidence.

- When cats panic, they lash out at anything between them and perceived safety, and stay aroused for at least an hour. Give frightened cats space, and don't talk, touch or follow her. Cat skin is so sensitive any contact can make the feelings of panic even worse.

- Speed up the recovery time by shutting out any further stimulation for at least 15 minutes. Turn off the lights in the room, draw the blinds, or toss a towel over the cat to muffle scary sounds.

- Comforting a scared cat with baby talk encourages the behavior to continue. Instead, praise and give treats for relaxed breathing, and calm expressions and body postures to help build confidence.

- Yelling and punishment could prompt fear aggression, so keep your temper. Low-pitched men's voices and heavier walk often sound scary to cats, so take care to "lighten" your tone and your step.

- Strong eye contact is a challenge that intimidates. Glance away while petting the cat and don't stare.

- When a scared cat hisses at your new boyfriend, his departure rewards Kitty and teaches her a fearful display works. Instead of leaving, encourage human guests to stay calm and sit quietly across the room so the cat can retreat instead.

- Shy cats fear hands if they've been abused. Others have a petting "threshold" and become aggressive. Instead of petting on the head, offer Sheba a closed fist or index finger to sniff, head butt and cheek rub.
- Play builds confidence in shy cats. Fishing pole style toys and flashlights allow people to interact at a "safe" distance that doesn't threaten the fearful cat, while teaching Sheba being near to you offers a fun benefit. Use both hands, a different toy in each, to engage both the shy cat and a resident cat at the same time to help teach them to get along.
- Use the pheromone product Feliway to help the cats feel more comfortable about their environment. The plug-in product helps all the cats "chill."
- Add several drops of the Rescue Remedy for all of your cats to sip, because it can help diffuse the other felines' aggression toward the shy kitty.
- Using the TTouch technique on the ears of shy cats can have a positive effect.
- Counter conditioning with incremental exposure to the trigger can help cats learn to tolerate scary situations. Stage "safe" exposures. For example, ask the (scary) child to stand across the other room while you give Kitty treats or play with a feather to reward her staying calm.
- Next, have the child stand a bit closer, or sit on the floor. If Kitty remains calm, offer another treat or game. Only go on to the next level when the cat remains okay with the last gradient.

VET ALERT!
HYPERTHYROIDISM

Middle aged and older cats may develop hyperthyroidism, an endocrine (hormonal) disease that revs up the metabolism. The condition caused by an over-active thyroid spills too much hormone into the cat's system. Affected cats have an increased appetite but lose weight, pace a lot, become short tempered, and often howl and yowl incessantly.

A blood test diagnoses the condition, which can be treated, controlled or even cured with ongoing drug therapy, surgery, or radioactive iodine treatment. Cats suffering from hyperthyroid disease often also have high blood pressure and/or kidney problems at the same time. Be sure to have your cat examined by a veterinarian, if she suddenly becomes hyperactive.

THE "ZOOMS" and MIDNIGHT MADNESS

For most cats, actual hyperactivity is rarely a problem and since cats normally sleep up to 16 hours a day they almost never have problems with insomnia. Felines naturally become most active at dawn and dusk, and nocturnal behaviors that keep you awake are most common in kittens and usually decrease when she reaches 12 to 18 months of age. While the nonstop energy of one cat challenges owners, a houseful of galloping felines multiplies the problem. The hijinks not only disturbs you especially at night, it can rub cranky cats the wrong way and prompt short tempers to flare, or teach bad habits to more sedate well behaved felines.

Some breeds are more active than others. Persians tend to be more sedate, while Abyssinians and Siamese swing from the drapes. When active cats don't have legal outlets for energy, they get creative and empty your sock drawer. You may reward unruly behavior without meaning to. If Sheba learns opening kitchen cupboards or vaulting to door tops garners attention, she'll continue the antics. The following tips can help put the brakes on your cat's non-stop activity.

- Cats sleep all day and want to play when you hit the sack. Prevent access to the cats' favorite sleeping places during the day, so they sleep at night.
- Tire the cats out in a constructive way and they'll leave your goldfish bowl alone. Twenty minutes aerobics twice a day works well. Schedule playtime a half hour before bedtime to tire your cats out so they'll sleep when you do.
- Feed your cats just before you go to bed to keep them from waking up hungry and pestering you at 3 a.m. to fill the bowl. You can put their last meal of the day in several "treat balls" filled with favorite kibble, so they must play and manipulate the ball to shake food out to eat.

- Harp music works as a natural, non-drug sedative but any slow, calm, instrumental music arrangement can be soothing. Special arrangements touted as "Pet Music" may be helpful for your cat.

- The brain manufactures the hormone melatonin, which acts like a time-keeper to tell us when to sleep and when to wake up, and can help lull cats to sleep. Melatonin is available at health food stores— ask your vet for the proper dosage.

- Milk contains the chemical tryptophan that helps promote sleep, and a quarter cup warm milk per cat may help your felines snooze more readily. However, some cats don't digest milk easily so lay off the treat if diarrhea develops.

- When your new kitten pesters the adult felines in the house, adopting a second kitten closer to her age can more effectively wear her out.

- Smart, active cats relish training, which gives them something constructive to do with their brains. Find a behavior she already does, such as reach out with a paw toward the feather. Reward the behavior with a favorite treat, and you've taught her to "wave." Teaching one cat in front of the others prompts copycat behavior once they realize the "wave" gets a treat.

- Highly motivated cats hate being ignored and settle for your angry words if they can't get good attention. If you feed her to make Sheba stop biting your nose to wake you, she's trained you to fill the bowl. Only reward good behavior. Teach Sheba she must pay for attention, food, or anything she wants with something YOU want, such as a quiet "sit." If she yowls, the food stays in the can.

VET ALERT!
FELINE SENILITY

As cats age, sight and hearing fade and they can become disoriented at night. A nightlight helps them more easily find their way around, and calms the jitters so they sleep more soundly. Some very old cats develop memory problems similar to those suffered by human Alzheimer's patients.

Signs include disorientation, interaction changes (with people/other pets), sleep cycle changes, housetraining lapses, and anxiety. We can't stop aging changes, but a percentage of cats suffering from these cognitive disorders are helped with drug and/or nutritional therapy prescribed by the veterinarian.

- The drug Anipryl (selegiline hydrochloride) is FDA-approved for treatment of canine cognitive disorder, and helps up to 70 percent of dogs. It has also been used off-label to help cats with similar cognitive disorders.
- Cholodin-Fel, a nutritional supplement, contains choline and phosphatidylcholine that helps brain cells work more efficiently, and may benefit cats with cognitive dysfunction. Find more information at www.mvplabs.com

MOVING ANGST

Cats love routine so much, that change leaves them outraged. Moving traumatizes many cats because they so strongly bond to territory and place. Those upset over a move often act out by scratching more, and spraying urine to mark the new territory. Shy kitties may disappear for days or even weeks, until they feel more comfortable with the new surroundings, and will worry themselves sick if you aren't careful. Plan ahead to calm cat fears and make the transition go as smoothly as possible.

- Schedule your move when you can be at home with the cats and spend several days together. Don't leave the cats alone to deal with fears by themselves.
- Move cats in carriers to prevent them from accidentally escaping during the trip or upon arrival. Refer to Crate Expectations section for more tips.
- Once at the new house, confine the cats that get along to a single room, and shut the door. That keeps them safe while you unpack, arrange furniture, and open and shut doors. If you have a large number of felines, you may need two safe rooms.
- Help the cats feel more at home by bringing all the familiar toys, cat furniture, bowls and litter boxes along. Set these up in the safe room(s) to create a familiar "home base" they can become used to

very quickly. Your cats should stay confined in the room for at least the first two or three days until you see they feel comfortable in THAT room.

- Add Rescue Remedy to the cats' drinking water to relieve feline stress.

- Once the cats have cheek rubbed territory in their safe room, and act reasonably calm, open the door and allow them to explore at their leisure. Cats tend to take it slow and easy, checking out new territory a room at a time. If any of your cats don't get along, give pariah cats the opportunity to explore alone first, then switch out the more confident cats, before giving all the felines free rein in the new digs.

- Return to your old routine as soon as possible. It may be a new house, but a familiar feeding time, play periods, and your comings and goings should help remind the cats all's well in their world.

- Extra exercise calms cats during the transition period. Playing with them reassures that all is well. Tired cats also sleep more soundly and will be less stressed.

- If you plan to allow your cat outside, you MUST keep her confined indoors for at least one month. Cats let outside too soon after a move try to find their way back to their old home and become lost, injured or killed along the way. It takes time for Sheba to swear allegiance to the new residence, and to learn all the important feline landmarks inside the house and out. The first few visits outdoors are best done on a leash, until the cat has mind-mapped the area for herself and you are confident she can find her way back for dinner.

FEELING LONELY

Separation anxiety results when sensitive cats are apart from human loved ones, and most often happens when you spend less time with your cats due to a job change or vacation. In one study, of the cats with this condition, 90 percent had owners who worked long hours. In 80 percent of the cats, owner absence due to a vacation triggered the behavior or increased the frequency of problems. About ¼ of the affected cats had been adopted from a shelter at less than three months of age. As a consequence, these kitties formed much stronger attachments to one or more family member.

Classic signs include urinating and defecating on owner-scented objects, and some cats cry and become upset as you prepare to leave while others don't seem to notice your departure, but "act out" once left alone. Even if only one of your cats reacts to your absences with poor behaviors, separation anxiety affects the entire feline family because hit-or-miss bathroom behaviors upset the status quo. Having other buddy cats may help the lonely feline feel less upset, but usually the anxious cat needs you to feel happy again and a furry substitute won't do. Use behavior modification to help Sheba feel better.

- Most problem behaviors take place within twenty minutes after you leave, and how long you are gone doesn't seem to matter. Distract Sheba during this critical period so she won't dirty your bed by asking another family member to play interactive games with a fishing pole toy.

- About 1/3rd of cats react strongly, another 1/3rd react mildly, and the last 1/3rd don't react at all to catnip. If your feline goes bonkers for this harmless herb, leave a catnip treat to keep her happy when you leave. Food oriented cats can be distracted with a food-puzzle toy stuffed with a favorite treat.

- Cats that have been outside and seen the real thing often don't react, but homebody indoor-only cats enjoy watching videos of fluttering birds, squirrels and other critters. There are a number of these videos available, including the original called "Video Catnip."

- Cats pay attention to their surroundings, so playing familiar music that they associate with your presence can help ease the pain of you being gone. Specialized tunes such as Pet Melodies include nature sounds and Theta brain wave frequencies designed to calm pets.

- Desensitize your cats to the presence of the overnight bag by leaving it out all the time, so Sheba won't get upset when she sees you pack. Toss a catnip mouse inside the suitcase, and turn it into a kitty playground to help her identify the suitcase with positives, rather than your absence.

- Use behavior modification techniques so the triggers lose their power. Pick up the car keys 50 times a day, and then set them down. Carry your purse over your arm for an hour or more. When you repeat cues often enough, Sheba will stop caring about them and will remain calm when you do leave.

- Fake your departure by opening the door and going in and out twenty or more times in a row until Sheba ignores you altogether. Then extend your "outside" time to one minute, three minutes, five minutes and so on before returning inside. This gradual increase in absence helps build the cat's tolerance.

Chapter 7
SUPPERTIME

Cats live longer these days because of properly prepared commercial foods, but not all of these work for every cat. Commercial foods fit the needs of broad categories of cats, including growth for kittens, maintenance for adult cats, and a "senior" category for aging kitties. As kittens and cats mature, they must transition to the food that best fits their particular life stage.

Some cats may require a "therapeutic" diet, such as for kidney disease or weight loss/control, dispensed by prescription from the veterinarian. Appetite is a barometer of your cat's health. A sudden increased appetite, for example, may indicate hyperthyroid disease while a loss of appetite may point to intestinal blockage or any of a number of other physical or emotional health issues.

SNUBBING THE BOWL

Anorexia—refusing to eat—or a reduced appetite over the long term can be deadly. A wide range of health challenges can make Sheba finicky, and the most common—upper respiratory infection—is so contagious that multiple cats can get sick at the same time. Cats won't eat if their noses stop up and they can't smell their food.

Territorial issues between cats also impact the feline appetite. Stressful interactions make shy cats fearful so they avoid communal dining and miss out on the goodies. Dominant cats can guard the feeding station, so that even when kibble remains in the bowl, the intimidated felines don't dare approach.

Cats sometimes go through the motions of covering food the same way they cover waste in the litter box. They scratch the floor next to the food dish over and over again. This behavior can mean one of two things. Cats sometimes cover up rejected food in the same way they bury urine or feces. But other times, the scratching and covering may simply be caching behavior. Feral cats have occasionally been observed retrieving uneaten food that's been covered up.

When you feed all the cats free choice (from a single ever-full bowl) it can be hard to tell which cats have problems. The smallest or youngest cats in the home may not be able to eat all they need at one meal, especially if they must compete with a glutton who gobbles up everything ahead of them.

Pay attention to how much EACH cat eats, if they show up for dinner or hide, and whether they feel "bony" under all that fur. Appetite loss goes beyond a finicky attitude. There are a number of techniques you can use to prompt Kitty's appetite to return.

- Offer soft foods cats with mouth pain can eat, until a veterinary dentist can be seen. Up to 75 percent of all cats develop some form of dental disease by the time they reach two years old.
- Use a warm wet cloth to clean off gummy noses so sick cats can smell their food.
- Create a steamy room to aid the stuffy cats' breathing. Moist heat helps open up the clogged nose.
- Warm up leftover canned food in the microwave to mouse/prey body temperature. Heating helps unlock odors and makes food more pungent and more appealing.
- Moisten dry kibble with warm water or low-fat no-salt chicken broth to spark your cats' appetite.
- Offer a top dressing of soft foods or meat baby food on the cat's regular diet. Canned and gourmet diets include more fat and flavor enhancers that tempt the reluctant eater, and human baby foods also appeal to sick cats. Avoid foods that contain onion, which can be problematic for cats.
- Leaving the food out all the time works for cats able to self-regulate and not over-eat, but can wear out the "appetite" centers of sick

cats so Sheba loses her appetite. Offer small amounts every hour with a break in between times.

- When a gobbler out-eats nibblers, or a dominant cat keeps shy felines from feeding, set up more than one feeding station and serve meals separately. Look for more tips for dealing with these problems in the section titled "The Kitty Smorgasbord."
- Cats fed the same diet throughout their life may not recognize the new kibble as edible. Gradual transition from the old to the new food works best. Mix ¼ of the new diet with ¾ of the old for a week. The second week, mix the two diets 50/50. The third week, mix ¾ of the new with ¼ of the old until finally Sheba eats 100 percent of the new food.
- Feed Sheba from your finger while stroking her neck to stimulate her to eat. Pungent foods like tuna work best to tempt flagging feline appetites, and in cases of long term anorexia, it's "legal" to offer the cat anything just to get her to eat.

VET ALERT!

Cats that stop eating for even a day or two can become very ill when the condition affects the liver. Fatty liver disease (hepatic lipidosis) may result when the body reflexively moves fat stores into the liver to counter the lost nutrition. The stored fat interferes with liver function, and makes the cat feel even sicker and less willing to eat. This creates a vicious cycle and in some cases, the kitty must be hospitalized and a feeding tube inserted to be force fed, before she'll regain her appetite.

THE KITTY SMORGASBORD

Different personalities, social interactions, and health issues will impact appetite, diet and feeding schedule and dictate how to manage the multiple cat home. When cats are approximately the same age, the same diet may be appropriate. But when they are different ages you may need one for kittens, for instance, or a senior formulation for your aging crew.

The more cats you have, the greater the chance they'll require different foods. One adult may need a food to control lower urinary tract problems, which won't work for the new kitten. Another cat eats reduced calorie food, while his best cat-buddy requires a high-protein diet to control diabetes. Feeding multiple diets becomes a management issue of time, space, and personalities. Feel free to use one, all, or any combination of tips to design the best situation for your cats.

- It can be overwhelming to keep track of multiple cats during dinner, but no rule says they must all be fed at once. Staggered feedings even 10 minutes apart may allow you to supervise each meal, and "ride herd" on the kitties who shouldn't nibble from a particular formula.
- Make sure the cats' bowls are a safe distance apart, so they don't feel their personal space has been invaded. Cats form good opinions of each other by eating within sight of one another, because that creates a positive association for them. If a cat stops chewing to stare at another feline, move the bowls further apart.
- Cats that seem to guard feeding stations, or that seem fearful to eat when another kitty is present, will require separate areas to eat.
- Some felines love to scrounge, "hunt" or swipe food, so give these cat burglars a legal outlet. Treat balls dispense a single meal to one cat, or treats to a group so as the cat plays, the dry food inserted into the ball or toy dispenses a kibble at a time. That keeps Sheba fed and entertained, and out of another feline's bowl.
- Garfield gluttons can't resist grazing from other cats' bowls. As sign a single bowl for each cat and an individual place for each bowl. Cats faithful to a routine are less likely to interrupt each other's mealtimes. Countertops, tables, various levels on the cat tree, or book shelves all offer valuable kitty real estate for individual feeding locations each cat can "own."

- Aged arthritic cats have more trouble reaching second-story locations. Set the food bowls of more agile cats on countertops out of reach of the geriatric feline who must eat a special diet.

- Food that gets gulped down too quickly often comes back up just as easily. Slow glutton cats by spreading kibble on a large flat pan, so the cat must "chase" it to get each piece. There are also commercial foods that make the kibbles or particles larger so the cat must chew, and can't gulp and swallow mouthfuls at a time.

- When cats of different sizes must eat two specific diets, such as a weight-reducing food for the big guy and a regular food for the little one, separate cats during meals in different rooms or create a 'boxed lunch.' Cut a tiny cat-size opening in a cardboard or plastic storage box to fit the smaller cat, and place the small cat's food bowl inside the box, where he can access and nibble at his leisure.

- Arthritic or overweight cats often require different foods than young athlete cats. A baby gate can segregate feeding stations by allowing only the more nimble cats to pass through or jump over.

- Pet doors with electronic "key" collars work well. The cat wearing the special collar or microchip can access the door into the screened porch to eat, for example, while the rest of the furry crew can't get through.

Chapter 8
CAT TO CAT INTRODUCTIONS

Adopting a mom with one or two kittens can offer security and build confidence particularly for the kittens. Similarly, adopting two kittens together can help them have a "buddy" to depend on for fun and games, and a furry security blanket when they feel fearful or stressed. But when you have an existing cat family, choose the new cat carefully, so she will fit into your existing feline family.

Because cats become so dependent upon routine, and bond closely with "place," bringing a new feline into the mix disrupts the worlds of both the resident cats and the new cat. Pay special attention to your current feline family. They've been around the longest, and their happiness must be considered first before any interloper's.

Existing cat hierarchies do not welcome strange felines with open paws. It's natural for your resident cats to try and drive off newcomers, or at least keep them at bay. Adding another kitty to the mix rarely solves existing behavior problems, either, and may make them worse or prompt new ones. A newcomer has a hard time being accepted under the best conditions, so keep these issues in mind to make the introductions run smoothly.

CAT COM*PET*ABILITY

There are five important components to consider when choosing a new feline to join your resident cats. You can refer to the LEASH acronym and discussion for details. Introductions take a great deal of patience, and you'll earn fewer gray hairs if your resident kitties already have basic manners, such as understanding the word "no."

If your current cat family gets along well, that improves the odds they'll welcome yet another feline to the mix because they already understand "cat language" and know how to fit into feline society. Adult cats more readily accept babies that don't challenge their social position. It's best to pick a kitten that's at least 12 to 16 weeks old so she's had time to learn important cat lessons from siblings and mom.

Cats reach "social maturity" by age four and often become very set in their ways, so if they've never before lived with another cat, extra patience will be needed to convince them to accept a newcomer. Watch the cat's tail and ears for cues. A low held or swishing tail reveals agitation, and ears turned to the side or backwards indicate fear and/or aggression. Be prepared to break up serious altercations that include growls or hisses, and separate the cats.

All cats need space to claim as their own. Ideally, have no more cats than you have bedrooms—or, build UP the potential territory by adding vertical space. If your cats get along and each has claimed a favorite resting/lookout spot, be sure to add several more options to accommodate the new felines. Don't expect cats to share with the new guy. They might become fast friends and want to sleep together, but that's a bonus if it happens, and not something to count on.

While you know all your resident cats, the new feline feels insecure and defensive. Sheba won't be willing to meet anybody until she's familiar and comfortable with the new environment. To be fair, initial introductions should be one-on-one, a single new cat meeting a single resident cat. ALWAYS pay more attention to the resident pet. The resident kitty will be much more willing to accept a newcomer as long as your affections aren't usurped. Be patient. It may take days, weeks or even months for the cats to get along. Rarely, it's love at first sight, but some cats may never become friends.

STEP-BY-STEP INTRODUCTIONS

These basic principles of introduction apply no matter what types of cats share your home and heart. The assumption has been made that both the resident(s) and the new kitty are confident, healthy felines that have been properly socialized. Extra steps may be necessary to smooth upset feelings when one or more of the cats involved have a physical or emotional health issue

Be sure that your resident "king cat" gets fed first, petted first, groomed first, and receives preferential treatment over lower-ranking cats. Preferred attention to a lower-ranking cat may inspire Sheba to kick furry tail to teach the lower ranking cat her place. If your top feline is geriatric, you may need to separate her during feeding and resting times so she's not bothered by a more energetic newcomer. Don't be surprised if neither the resident "king" nor the interloper end up on top. Adding a new feline could create a brave new kitty world and a fresh hierarchy as well.

- Neutering makes a cat's urine smell differently, and visiting the veterinarian also creates a "foreign" smell on the treated cat. Neuter new cats BEFORE beginning introductions or you'll have to start over after the vet visit.
- New cats feel more secure when initially confined to small areas of the house they more quickly get used to. Create a home base for the new cat in a small room with a door that shuts completely. If you have more than one new cat and they already know each other, you may be able to confine them together and they'll comfort and give confidence to each other.
- Cats become more upset by the sight of a strange feline than by the smell or sound. A solid door allows cats to meet via sound, smell, and paw pats under the door, yet avoid emotional overload prompted by restricting sensory input.
- The home base also keeps resident kitties happy that only a small portion of their territory has been invaded. Choose a room they normally don't use and won't feel as upset at being banned.
- Second-hand supplies that already smell like other cats make a new feline feel more insecure so stock the home base with only thoroughly washed food and water bowls, new toys, and a new scratching post and litter box. If your newcomer came with a favorite bed or toys, include these so the familiar smells help keep her calm. Include hiding places, such as cat tunnels, so she feels more secure about navigating the strange new room.
- Some initial posturing and hissing at the door is normal, and resident cats may engage in redirected aggression toward each other when they can't reach the newcomer. Cats tell you when they feel comfortable and are ready for the next step. Be encouraged by paw

pat games under the door, the new cat's willingness to come out of hiding and interact with you, and your resident kitties maintaining their normal routine and not aggressing toward companion cats.

- To further gauge your cats' readiness for a face-to-face, introduce individual cat scents to them. Bring something out of the home base that's scented by the new cat for the resident felines to smell, and vice versa. When you're dealing with a total of two or three kitties, a plate of food where each ate works well, because it also has a positive food association. DON'T switch bedding or the cats may urinate on it to show dominance. Hissing and growling after sniffing means they need more time segregated, but mild interest means you're on the right track.

- When you have more than three cats to introduce, use individual cloths or socks to collect cheek pheromones (one cloth per cat) by petting each cat's cheek. Take a cheek-rubbed cloth from the friendliest, most laid back of your resident kitties and leave that with the new cat for her to acclimate to one feline at a time—the one least likely to cause problems. Continue the scent exchange several times a day, offering only one resident cat "smell" to the newcomer at a time, until all the cats have had opportunity to become familiar with signature odors.

- Another way to share the scent between cats is to place a bit of the wet litter from the new cat's box in the resident kitties' facilities, and vice versa. Only use a tiny amount (think in terms of a pinch!) or you risk prompting box avoidance.

- A new cat won't want to meet anybody nose to nose until she feels secure in the surroundings. Once hissing fades, paw pats increase, or the kitties act disinterested, isolate all your resident cats in another room of the house. Then open the door to allow Sheba to wander around the rest of the house, cheek rub everywhere and "map" the location of all the good hiding places.

- Once the new cat has explored the rest of the house, place her in a carrier or another area of the house to allow your resident felines to check out her room. Don't force them into the new cat's home base, simply open the door. They may investigate all at once, in shifts, or some may ignore the invitation altogether.

- After your new cat feels comfortable navigating your house, open the door with no fanfare, and carefully (and silently) watch what happens. Remember, these initial introductions should be between the new cat and only ONE of your resident cats at a time (the friendliest first) and not the whole furry crew at once.

- Eating distracts both cats from the scary newness of the other animal, while associating food with each other's presence, so feed both cats during these initial meetings. Set food down in the new cat's room and offer the resident cat a meal at the same time outside the open door.

- Play builds confidence in shy cats, and can also associate fun times with the presence of the other feline. During initial meetings, have a second family member play with the new cat while the resident feline's favorite person plays with him. With practice, you can learn to manipulate a fishing pole or other interactive toy in each hand, to wrangle two cats at once. ALWAYS use two toys, or the cats may compete for the single lure and develop negative associations.

- Cats that live together and get along well create a group scent by sleeping together and grooming each other. New cats are shunned because they smell foreign and scary. Speed up introductions by making all the cats in the household smell alike. When dealing with only two cats, trade the collars they wear. For multiple resident cats, rub a towel over each cat in turn and then rub the new cat with the same towel. Alternatively, you can use a strong, pleasant scent like vanilla extract, a favorite perfume, or cologne, and dab just a tiny bit underneath the chin and at the base of the tail of each cat.

- It's normal for cats to approach each other, circle a bit, and each attempt to sniff the other's flank and tail region before moving to the head. Watch for tail language. A tail-up greeting from either cat signals friendly intensions. If both do this, thank your lucky stars. Chances are the introductions will go smoothly. Hisses and growls mean you should cut the session short and send the new cat back to home base.

- Use the pheromone product Feliway to signal cats that their environment is safe.

- The herbal product, Bach Flower Rescue Remedy also helps ease the emotional upheavals and you'll need to use it for two weeks to see a benefit.

- Add to an existing routine by incorporating the new kitty. Group activities like grooming or playing with a fishing pole lure toy are particularly helpful.

- Build confidence in all the cats by adding hiding places, scratching opportunities, and litter boxes so they don't have to argue over the facilities. Cat tunnels work great to give shy felines "hidden" pathways across the middle of rooms or long hallways so they feel protected while traveling to dinner or the bathroom.

- Until you're satisfied everyone gets along, the new cat should stay in her home base whenever you can't directly supervise. Replace the door with stacked baby gates so the cats can still interact through the mesh.

- Once cats begin sleeping or playing together, consider introductions over the hump. Be prepared to interrupt play that gets wild before it becomes aggression.

- Should aggression develop, start the introduction process all over again. Refer to the Cat-egorical Aggression chapter for more details.

GREEN-EYED MONSTERS

We can't know for sure if cats feel jealous emotions the same as humans, but for purposes of discussion that's how we'll refer to the behavior. Cats also often act jealous when a new boyfriend or baby steals their thunder. Just one cat with her tail in a twist can upset the rest of the feline family and make them suspicious of the person, or act poorly with feline companions.

The jealous cat's behavior changes confuse the other felines and make them act out as a result. In the most serious cases, jealousy escalates to aggression when cats seek to throw the interloper out of the house. Keep the peace with proper introductions to new people in your life.

- Cats become jealous when they think they might lose your love, so make a point of spending special time with them even when you have a new beau or baby. Either keep the old schedule the same as before, or introduce changes gradually so the cats can cling to that familiarity.

- You are the most important territory for your cats, but they also feel proprietary about the house. Make sure your cats feel safe and relaxed in a favorite place, such as on a cat tree, so they feel in control rather than fearful or defensive during introductions to new people.

- When your cats get along well, they can give each other confidence and friendly kitties can act as role models for the shy felines during these introductions. One-on-one introductions with the new human can be more intimidating for a single cat so initial meetings can be informal group gatherings.

- Cats do best when allowed to approach new people themselves. Ask guests to avoid eye contact and ignore the cat. That does more to spark kitty curiosity and an urge to investigate. If she check-rubs his pant leg, that's very positive.

- Cats identify friends and family members by their scent. Use a bit of your favorite perfume, cologne, or vanilla extract, or spray Feliway on guests' pant cuffs or ankles, to make new people smell like you, somebody your cats already love. Also dab a bit of the perfume or cologne on the back of the cats' necks and at the base of their tails so they smell like the "scary stranger" and won't be so fearful.

- The person who controls the resources garners trust and respect, so a new girlfriend, stepchild or spouse makes lots of points with cats by feeding them. Let your girlfriend fill the cats' bowls, but then leave so her presence doesn't keep the cats from eating.

- Play therapy can be a powerful bonding tool between humans and cats. New people can use fishing pole style toys and flashlights which are feline favorites because they can play from a safe distance.

- Banishing cats from the room or ignoring them in favor of the new person tells them they must compete for your attention. Instead, give cats EXTRA attention whenever the new person is nearby.

Cat-to-Baby Introductions

The old wives' tale that cats "suck the breath" of infants has no merit, and cats and babies can become great friends. They also have the potential to terrorize and/or injure each other. In order to have the best possible relationship, proper introductions matter. When you are expecting a new baby (or grandchild or visiting infant), prepare your cats in advance to help ensure the encounter goes smoothly.

Cats that get their tails in a twist over newcomers to the family can take out their angst on each other, you, or the furniture (with claws and urine, for example). Knowing what to expect and how to manage it can prevent the worst problems. It's much easier to prevent than to try and eliminate existing behaviors.

Most cats feel curious about infants, and may seek out that warm body and try to use Baby as a warm bed. A baby's milky breath smells good and tempts many kitties to take a sniff. Although a confident cat may tolerate infants, toddlers often scare cats when they chase, pull tails, and make weird high-pitched noises. Don't expect every cat to react the same way. Some may love being loved by the visiting toddler while others dive under the bed for the duration.

Consider your cats' feelings, especially if she has never before been around children. Compared to adults, babies and toddlers are Martians and particularly daunting because they don't yet understand and take direction as well as older children. Kids smell different than adults, have high-pitched funny voices, move in unpredictable ways, and appear threatening. Babies that crawl may mimic prey behavior in their sounds and actions. Wary cats may switch into stranger-danger mode and either become frightened and hide, or defensive and try to drive away the scary creature. Neither option is good.

Before Baby Comes Home

Prepare for the nine months before the infant comes home. Cats love the status quo so make any changes gradually.

- Let Them Explore. Allow your cats to investigate the redecorated nursery so they won't feel left out. This is especially true if the cats have previously had free access to the room—banning them may cause behavior issues when they act out from the stress. Before the baby arrives is a good time to learn how your cats react to new furniture. For example, many cats think the new baby bed or basinet is just for them, and consider the butterfly mobile a fun cat toy.
- Manage Access. Install a baby gate in the doorway so your cats can see into the room and be a part of the joy but are kept out when you can't supervise their action. Placing a plastic carpet protector, nub side up, on the mattress will shoo most cats away.

- Practice Crying. Fussy babies sound similar to kitten distress cries or even prey so it can be upsetting for cats to hear this. Record infant cries and play back to your cats to acclimate them to the sounds. Cats may ignore the sound or act curious, and reward either behavior with calm praise.

- Offer Positive Associations. Should your cats act upset with a hiss, growl or hiding, associate the baby noises with something they like. For instance, play a game of feather tag or offer a treat before you switch on the noise so your cats are already in a happy frame of mind. Play the sound for five seconds at a time, and slowly increase the time frame as long as the cats stay calm.

- Dab On Baby Smells. Begin wearing baby powder or lotion weeks in advance so your cats associate the aromas with a beloved and safe human they already know.

- Adjust Your Schedule. A new baby throws your old routine out the window. Prepare your cats in advance so they aren't totally thrown when you attend the baby first thing in the morning instead of running to fill their food bowl. Be sure to include CAT TIME in the schedule so they don't feel totally neglected. While you're understandably happy, excited (and exhausted!) with a new baby in the house, excluding your cat friends from your joy only confuses them at best. At worst, upset cats act out when stressed with aggression toward each other or other stress-reducing behaviors like urinating inappropriately.

- Give Cats An Advance Sniff. When the baby finally arrives bring home something scented with the infant so that your cat has an advance introduction. Since cats identify "friends" as smelling familiar and similar to them, it will be helpful to offer sniffing opportunities ahead of introductions. Bring home a tee shirt or baby blanket.

- "Sock" Your Cats. No, I don't mean to hit them—simply take a pair of baby socks and pet your cats' cheeks so the footwear contains the feline "safe" pheromones that keep cats calm about their territory. Then have the baby wear the socks, and voila! Your baby now smells like part of the cats' family group with the communal scent, and your pets will more readily recognize the infant as a safe and acceptable member of the household.

When Baby Comes Home

When you bring home the baby, treat the event in a matter-of-fact manner, and don't make a big deal of the introduction (even though it's momentous, of course!). You want the kitty to understand this is a normal, expected part of her life.

- Act Normal. Don't force the introduction. But if the cat acts interested, allow her to sniff the baby's foot, perhaps (with that scented sock). By allowing your cat to actually look at, smell, and touch that creature that's so very different, she'll understand there's nothing to fear.
- Reward Calm Cat Confidence. Praise cats when they act well, and ignore shy or fearful behavior.
- Associate Good Things. Cats quickly learn to associate the baby with what's important to them—if they get ignored or yelled at when the infant is near, the baby will acquire negative associations. Figure out what your cats love and link it to the baby's presence. Maybe you can toss treats or play with the laser toy when the baby naps on your lap, for instance.

Cats to Kid/Toddler Introductions

Once babies start walking they can become more interesting—and challenging—for your cats. Many of the same cat-to-baby introductions apply, but in addition, refer to these tips for toddlers and older children.

- Offer Elevated Perches. As long as your cats have second-story territory like cat trees and chair backs out of the child's reach, they generally can stay above the fray. Cats often enjoy the show from on high once they know crawling babies and high-energy kids can't catch them.
- Provide A Safe Retreat. Be sure your cats have a kitty sanctuary that's off limits to kids. Even pets that adore children need private time and a place to go that they know they won't be pestered.

- Teach Kids Limits. Ask toddlers to practice petting a stuffed toy or the child's own arm or head. Young kids take time to learn that cats can be hurt and lash out from pulled tails or ears.

- Practice Purr-Speak. High pitched screams could potentially prompt the cats to aggress toward each other or the child. Challenge children to talk to cats in a whis-PURR voice that entices cats to come near for pets. You can explain that just like children can get frightened of scary sounds, cats can be fraidy-cats and it takes very talented kids to know how to be cat-friendly.

- Ignore The Cats. Staring is a challenge that can hiss off cats. But when ignored, felines typically can't resist investigating on their own. So challenge your toddler or older child to an "ignore the cat" game, and see how long they can pretend the kitty isn't there. In most cases, a confident feline will eventually approach.

- Seat The Kids. Cats hate being chased, and toddlers love running after them. So make it a cat rule that kids must sit before they can touch. Once seated, the child can lure and entice the cats' interest and interaction with a feather toy or ribbon. Sitting in place and engaging with long-distance interactive toys tells cats they're safe—they won't be grabbed or chased—so they come closer and have fun. Playing builds a positive cat-child relationship that can grow into love.

- Offer Cat Treats. When cats still act reluctant to approach, find a smelly, tasty treat the cat loves but ONLY gets from the child. While sitting on the floor, the child should gently toss the treat to (not AT) the cat.

- Make A Point. Ask the child to try "pointing" a finger to the cats. This often seems to invite a feline nose-touch greeting.

Chapter 9
CAT-TO-DOG INTRODUCTIONS

Why do I include a section about introducing dogs? You're a cat lover, devoted to your clowder and they to you, right? Never say never, though. You may meet the love-of-your-life who GASP! already has a dog, and then what? You wouldn't want somebody to ask you to give up your beloved felines, nor should you expect someone to give up dog companions. Just in case, you'll find some tips for smoothing interspecies relationships. After all, cats are not dogs—and dogs are not cats—and introducing them takes a slightly different approach.

Most cats and dogs can get along famously, especially if properly socialized during puppy- or kittenhood. But it will take longer to introduce them if either or both have never had positive experiences with the other species. Your rate of success also depends on the pet personalities involved.

Some dog breeds tend to be more dangerous to cats simply because of their heritage. Terriers and sight hounds, for example, were bred to chase down prey, and the scurrying cat can trigger predatory aggression to chase, catch or even kill. A great disparity in size also has inherent risk even if the much bigger dog never intends harm. A St. Bernard might sit on and squash a tiny kitten by accident.

THE TEN COMMANDMENTS OF PET DYNAMICS

1. Introductions go much more smoothly when at least the resident pet already knows the rules of the house. At a minimum, they should understand "no" and dogs should be leash trained.
2. Cats and dogs properly socialized as youngsters to each other will be most likely to accept new pets as friends. When the mother dog accepts cats or the mother cat accepts dogs as friends, their offspring learns more readily to accept the other species as "family."
3. Resident adult pets more willingly accept babies, because they're less of a challenge to the adult's social status. Kittens more readily integrate into a dog home, and resident adult cats feel less threatened by puppy-size newcomers.
4. All pets need space to claim as their own. If you don't have enough rooms to accommodate them, enrich the environment by adding vertical space for the cats and a safe enclosed outdoor area for dogs.
5. Newcomer cats must be familiar with the new environment before willing to meet resident dogs.
6. Choosing complementary pet personalities promotes better relationships. An outgoing cat can build confidence in your shy dog.
7. Choose complementary activity types. A playful cat as a partner with your lap-sitting pooch can work well because neither infringes on the other's preferred way of life. An energetic pup also helps get the overweight couch-potato cat off her furry tail, while the sedate cat may have a settling influence on the brash dynamo.
8. Introduce the new pet to one resident animal at a time. It's not fair to subject them to the whole "gang" and it's more difficult for you to supervise more than a pair.
9. ALWAYS pay more attention to the resident pet when he or she is within view. The resident pet will be much more willing to accept a newcomer as long as your affections aren't usurped.
10. Be patient. It may take days, weeks or even months for the pets to accept each other and get along. Some pets may never become friends, and the best you can hope for is tolerance or avoidance.

STEP-BY-STEP INTRODUCTIONS

Introducing your cat and dog to each other may immediately result in love at first sight, or more commonly will take time for the pair to accept each other. Follow the steps below when both the resident(s) and the new pet are confident, healthy animals that have been properly socialized as pups or kittens.

Dog-to-dog introductions are best begun on "neutral" territory, which often means the park or a neighbor's yard. But plunking the cat down in a carrier or on a leash in the middle of a park spells disaster on a grand scale! Therefore, dog-to-cat introductions must take place in your home in a similar fashion to cat-to-cat introductions, with accommodations made for the sensitivities of the dog and cat involved.

Watch your pets' body language to gauge their feelings. A tail-up greeting from the cat indicates a friendly approach, while a canine play-bow, an easy-going wag, and perhaps a yawn or two or rolling on his back says Rex means no harm. Delay the next step if you see the cat swish her tail or pin her ears flat to her head—that means she's fearful and may become aggressive. Dominant dogs may place a paw on the cat's back, or signal aggression with raise hackles, or a snarl.

Take care to curb the new baby pet's enthusiasm. Puppies and kittens may not understand the "keep back!" signals of the older resident pet, so make sure the adults have enough room to get away to avoid a defensive snap. Containing clueless youngsters inside pet carriers, or on leashes, can be helpful. On the plus side, gregarious pups and juvenile cats don't discourage easily and often wear down curmudgeonly residents, as long as you run interference and ensure safety.

Adult-to-multiple-adult introductions take the longest because each "pair" must meet individually, and work out his or her own feelings about the interloper. Dogs tend to follow your lead, so make it clear you welcome the newcomer and your resident canine crew will be more accepting of the new cat.

It's vital that your resident "top dog" or "king cat" be fed first, petted first, groomed first, and be given any other preferential treatment, to ensure peace and harmony in the multi-pet household. Never show preferred attention to an animal lower in the hierarchy; that simply prompts confusion and may inspire the "King" to put the lower ranking pet in his place. Old dogs or cats may need to have private feeding and resting times so they're not bothered by a more energetic newcomer.

The following techniques help ease introductions. New dogs that meet resident cats won't always require the same steps as when introducing a new cat to resident dogs, but some tips apply to both scenarios. You live with your animals and know them best, so use your good judgment to create a workable program. In almost all cases, it's best to take extra time rather than rush through the techniques, and don't be afraid to start from scratch if one of the animals needs this help.

FOR BOTH

- Spay or neuter the newcomer BEFORE introductions. Fixed dogs and cats aren't as great a threat to the status quo.
- Use pheromone products to calm the pets and reduce the stress of introductions. The plug-in products Feliway for cats and D.A.P. for dogs diffuse in the air to benefit all the pets, or spray D.A.P. on a kerchief for a particular dog to wear.
- Add a few drops of Rescue Remedy to the drinking water of the pets.
- Sequester the new pet in a single room with all the necessary kitty or doggy accoutrements. If a new pet came with a favorite bed or toy, be sure to include this in his room so that the old, familiar smells help keep him calm.
- Choose a room with a door that shuts completely such as second bedroom. Isolating the new pet tells your resident pet that only a small portion of the house has been invaded, not all the territory.
- Expect cats to posture or hiss and dogs to sniff, whine, growl or bark whether they're new pets or current residents. Feel encouraged once the barking and hissing fade, especially if the canine "play-bows" at the door or the pair play patty-cake-paws under the door.
- After the new pet has been in the room alone for a few days, and the hisses or growls have faded, bring out something the new pet has scented, such as a plate of food where she just ate, and allow your resident dog or cat to smell it.

INTRODUCING NEW CAT TO A RESIDENT DOG

- Put the dog in his yard out of sight while you bring the new cat into the house and leave her in her "isolation room." Problems are much less likely if a resident dog enters the house and finds the new kitty already there.

- Sequestering Sheba allows her to become used to the "domain" of the isolation room so she feels safe and has a home base. It also allows her to safely interact with the resident dogs with paw pats under the door. Simply put down her carrier, open it, and then leave the room so she can come out at her own pace.

- Once the hissing fades and the paw pats increase, allow your new cat to wander around the rest of the house while Rex stays outside in the yard. Don't force anything, simply open the isolation room door and let Sheba explore and "map" the location of all the good hiding places and high perches to feel safe.

- While Sheba explores one of the other rooms, let the resident dog check out the "safe room" to become more familiar with the new cat's smells.

- Next, install a baby gate in the isolation room so the cat and dog can meet at their own speed, but through the safety of the barrier. Pay attention to how each pet reacts before proceeding to the next step. You want to see confidence and interest, and if either pet shows shyness or aggression, give them more time. Refer to the "Fear and Shyness" section.

- If you don't have a baby gate, you can use a pet carrier to contain a confident new cat and/or the resident dog that's small or shy. DO NOT place a frightened cat in a carrier and allow a pushy dog to sniff, or you'll further traumatize her and delay any acceptance of the resident dog.

- Once Sheba feels comfortable navigating your house and meetings through the baby gate or carrier have gone well, prepare for whisker-to-whisker meetings. Avoid fanfare. Put the dog on a leash, and then open the baby gate and watch what happens. Remember to confine this introduction to the new cat and only one of your dogs, not everybody at once.

- Keep the pets away from closely confined spaces during initial meetings. An open room with lots of space reduces tension.

- Feed both pets during this initial meeting, on opposite ends of a room to distract them and also help them associate FOOD with each other's presence.

- If the pets aren't interested in food, engage them in play. Whoever your dog feels closest to should interact with the cat, so Rex sees that YOU accept the kitty and will be more willing to follow his beloved owner's example.

- Make your resident dog smell like the new cat. Sheba identifies friendly family members by their scent—and everyone smells alike when they like each other because of mutual grooming, and cheek rubbing behavior. The "vanilla trick" can work by dabbing a bit of vanilla extract—or your favorite cologne—on the back of the neck and base of the tail of both animals.

- Ensure feline perches are out of dog-sniffing range but within Sheba's reach.

- Interrupt sniffing every now and then by calling the dog away or guiding him with the leash. Keep these initial meetings short— about five to ten minutes—so you don't wear out the pets.

- If they start to play, great! Allow play for a few minutes, and then break up the games and end the session on a good note so they want more of each other.

- Continue to segregate the cat in her safe room whenever you cannot directly supervise the pair. Most cats can jump over the baby gate and regulate interactions, or you can place a stepstool for Sheba— or raise the baby gate just enough for her to wiggle beneath. Continue to offer more planned meetings for another week, monitoring the dog until he can control himself and respects the cat even when off leash.

INTRODUCING NEW DOG
TO A RESIDENT CAT

- Ask a friend to bring the new dog into the house out of sight of the resident cat so kitty won't associate you with the "scary" critter.

- Keep the isolation room door shut for at least the first week, and longer if necessary. Resident cats become upset at the sight of a stranger but may be curious about the smell or sound.

- Isolating Rex allows the resident cats to feel less threatened while learning to accept the new smells and sounds of that dog-behind-the-door.

- Schedule Rex's potty breaks to keep them from seeing each other too soon. Put Sheba in your bedroom during the dog's travels to and from the back yard.

- Offer Sheba the opportunity to check out the "safe room" while the dog is outside, to become more familiar with the dog's smells. Just leave the door open and she'll explore at her leisure, but don't force her into the room. Let it be the cat's idea.

- Next, replace the isolation room door with a baby gate so the pets can see each other, and sniff or paw pat through the opening while they're safely separated. Your cat can control the interaction by jumping over or winding through the baby gate, if she really feels the urge to check out Rex.

- If you don't have a baby gate, and the dog is small enough, you can place Rex inside a crate or pet carrier for the cat to approach in a safe, controlled way. Watch both pets' reactions closely and delay the next step until you are satisfied they feel comfortable.

- Put Rex on a leash before removing the baby gate, so he and the cat can finally meet. Remember, these initial introductions should be between the new pet and only ONE of your resident animals, not everybody at once.

- Keep Rex under leash control but give him some wiggle room or a tight leash can make him feel tense.

- Make initial meetings as pleasant as possible. If your cat feels proprietary toward you, engage her in a fishing pole game while another family member handles Rex, so that the cat associates the dog with good things for her. You can also give each animal a plate of food on opposite ends of a room, to distract them and reward the fact they ignore each other.

- Use a dab of vanilla extract—or your favorite perfume or cologne—and dab just a bit on the back at the base of the tail, and on the back of the neck of both pets to make them smell alike. Making the new dog smell like the cat goes a long way toward encouraging Sheba to accept him as a family member.

- Whenever possible make initial meetings in an open room with lots of space, and lots of cat second-story perches available. That way,

Sheba can check out the dog from her cat tree, well beyond nose-sniffing range, and feel more comfortable.

- Keep first nose-to-nose meetings to only five or ten minutes, and then give everyone a break and return the dog to his room.
- When the dog and cat willingly nose sniff, the cat cheek rubs the dog, and/or Rex play-bows an invitation to a game, that's great! Allow play for a few minutes at a time, but interrupt before either pet becomes overexcited.
- Continue to offer planned meetings for another week, monitoring the dog until he can control himself and respects the cat even when off leash.
- Segregate the new pet alone in his "safe room" whenever you are not able to directly supervise, until you are satisfied that the cat and dog get along well, and both have "safe places" they can retreat when necessary.

CUTTING THE CHASE

Some dogs can't resist chasing the cat, but Sheba doesn't appreciate being turned into a windup toy for the dog's amusement. Teaching Rex to refrain from the chase not only enforces good manners, but also becomes a safety issue.

You can train better doggy manners by placing a confident cat in a protective carrier, and then giving the dog treats for behaving calmly. Ask the dog to sit, heel, stay, or other obedience commands, and offer the BEST treats (a bonanza of a whole handful!) for moving away from the cat. Be aware, though, that such a situation can be highly traumatic for shy cats even if you treat Sheba as well.

A better technique for most cats uses classical conditioning. Just as Pavlov conditioned dogs to salivate when they heard a bell, you teach your dog to respond to the cat's presence in an acceptable manner. You'll need a leash, treats, the cat and dog, and lots of patience.

- Ensure the cat's safety by keeping your dog under leash control. Prevent ANY chase from taking place, because the activity feels so good to your dog he'll gladly ignore or give up any other type of reward. Even if the cat instigates the session (some cats tease dogs unmercifully), don't allow any chase or tag games until after the dog has learned proper manners.

- Have plenty of smelly, tasty treats handy, ready to reinforce your dog at the drop of a hat—or presence of a cat.

- Every time (and I mean EVERY time) the cat makes an appearance, give the dog a treat. Offer this reward whether he acts calm, excited, looks at the cat, barks or anything else. The equation should be: CAT'S PRESENCE = DOG TREAT. Use the leash only to keep him a safe distance from the kitty, not to force his attention or behavior into what you want him to do. Let his brain process the equation on its own time. Some dogs "get it" right away and others take longer.

- Within a few sessions, nearly every dog will start to look to you for a treat each time the cat appears. Rather than lunging and chasing instinctively, you've conditioned a new response: to expect a reward.

- Continue to reinforce this behavior for at least a week or two. Brush up with more training sessions as needed—for some dogs, that might be every month. Make sure the dog stays leashed and the pets separated when not supervised, until confident the new canine response has become ingrained.

PART THREE

COMMON MULTIPET FRUSTRATIONS

Chapter 10
PET PEEVES

Whether you have two cats or a dozen, chances are you will experience one or more of these top complaints. It's hard enough to train proper behavior to a single cat but sharing your house with many complicates how to deal with these issues. Companion critters can tempt clueless pets into causing trouble.

Cats don't behave badly to get your goat, though, and understanding what prompts these behaviors is the first step to finding a solution. The key is to make the objectionable behavior less appealing, and give the miscreant a better "legal" alternative.

Other times, the irksome behavior is perfectly normal and in cat language may even be a compliment or expression of affection. Understanding these puzzling feline antics not only helps owners learn how to better deal with frustration but also helps us appreciate our cats unique and endearing foibles.

BUTT PRESENTATION

Cat butt presentation is a part of cat talk and cats normally sniff each other's anal regions the same way people smile in greeting. Friendly cats also present their ass-ets to humans when they jump onto laps and turn around. Don't be upset—your cat is simply being polite.

When cats greet each other for the first time they sniff each other's face and neck as a sort of "hello there." This could be compared to you nodding a greeting to a stranger at first meeting. Sniffing this area also picks up pheromones that signal friendship. First sniffs to the cheeks actually help calm feelings of aggression or fear.

The second stage of meet-and-greet sniffing proceeds to sniffing flanks, which could be the equivalent to a human "nice to meet you" polite handshake. This is the area that holds family scent of other cat body rubs, grooming, or a human's petting hand so it tells the sniff-er quite a lot about the cat and relationships.

The final sniffing stage targets the anal region beneath the raised tail. The cat's signature scent is found here, and this scent tells cats about sexual status and reveals the most. Kitties that keep the tail down and don't want to be sniffed might be compared to a shy person hiding her face.

Since a raised tail signals, "I mean no threat," the combination of raised tail with offering a butt-sniffing opportunity is the equivalent of a human's enthusiastic hug or a kiss on each cheek in greeting.

Does the cat expect you to sniff? Probably not. As much as they love us, cats know we aren't cats. Still, the polite body language speaks volumes about how the cat feels about us. Offering a sniff signals great trust and affection. The cat butt sniff offer is a back-handed feline compliment.

Dumping her off your lap or otherwise snubbing the behavior can lead to the cat ignoring your overtures, as well. Cats tend to reciprocate affection when we do the same—a quid pro quo arrangement that benefits all involved. So when she presents butt, give your cat a scratch and entice her into another, more appreciated pose with a feather toy, for example.

CATERWAULING

Humans often overlook body language that makes up a great deal of cat communication, but feline yowls, growls, hisses and purrs get our undivided attention—especially at 5:00 a.m.

Not all cats are vocal. Persians and the beautiful blue Chartreux breeds, for instance, tend to be rather quiet while Siamese and Oriental-type breeds are especially talkative. One yodeler can get the whole furry crew caterwauling.

In multi-pet homes, troublemakers (other pets pestering) may prompt problem meowing. Cats introduced to other cats or dogs for the first time often meow more as a result. Felines use a wide range of vocalizations to communicate with other cats, but seem to reserve "meows" primarily for talking to their people. Meows are demands: let me OUT, let me IN, pet me, play with me, FEED me! As the cats become more passionate and insistent, meows grow more strident and lower-pitched.

Giving in to meow-demands tells Sheba that pestering works to get her way, and any response such as putting the pillow over your head, yelling at her, or pushing her off the bed still gives her the attention she craves. The only way to extinguish this behavior is to totally ignore the cat. That means, you DON'T get up to feed her; you DON'T indulge in toe-tag games; you DON'T yell at her, spray her with water, or give any attention at all. That's hard to do when she's paw-patting your nose, or shaking the windows with yowls. It can take weeks to months to get rid of this behavior once established, but with patience, it can be done.

- Invest in earplugs to help you ignore the cat's plea for attention.
- Many people enjoy sleeping with their cat until Sheba opens her meow-mouth. You may need to make a hard choice, and shut her out of the bedroom. Cats shut out of the bedroom often continue to pester from the other side of the door, and may even scratch or otherwise cause damage. Choose a "safe room" on the other side of the house stocked with lots of toys, a litter box, scratch object and food, and confine noisy cats out of earshot.
- If other cats or dogs instigate the meowing, separating and confining the problem fur-kid away from the others can help. When the dog stays in his crate for the night, he can't chase and tease the cat—or vice versa.
- Meowing can result from boredom. Offer a Treat Ball or other irresistible toy that keeps the cat's brain (and mouth) occupied so she won't meow.
- Closing windows so your cats can't hear or see outside strays may help. Anything that attracts roaming cats to visit during the night should be discouraged. For example, avoid leaving out food on the porch, and clean up brush piles that make attractive critter hiding places.

VET ALERT!

For some reason, cats tend to become more vocal when suffering from hypertension (high blood pressure), which can be a result of kidney or heart disease. Excessive meowing also may be a sign of deafness in aging cats. When Sheba can't hear her own voice any longer, she tends to meow louder and longer. Check with your veterinarian about excessive meowing in any cat.

CHEWING HABITS

Dogs chew to explore their world, manipulate objects, to relieve boredom, and because it feels good, and they always target your most prized possessions as chew toys because they smell like you. Puppies and kittens test their world the same way human infants do—everything goes into the mouth, and while cats usually outgrow the teething stage, adult dogs retain the chew habit. Oddly enough, some felines fixate on paper, and nibbling kitties show a talent for creating confetti works of art from cardboard boxes.

Chewing not only damages property when pets target illegal objects, it can break teeth, result in dangerous swallowed objects or deadly electrocution should Sheba gnaw the computer wire. Don't blame the pet for doing what comes naturally. Instead, prevent problems by reducing opportunities to make mistakes.

- Pet proof the house by picking up tempting objects and confining the chewer to a "safe" zone when you can't supervise her activity. A product such as Bitter Apple applied to forbidden electrical cords helps train cats to leave dangerous items alone. If your cats like the taste of Bitter Apple, use menthol scented Vicks Vapo-Rub and paint baseboards or apply to cloth draped over forbidden targets to keep pets at bay.
- When you catch your cat chewing a forbidden object, offer a legal chew toy such as a rawhide chew for small dogs. Soak one in warm

water or broth and zap with the microwave for ten seconds to soften the leather and make it more pungent, so it appeals to cat cravings.

- Cats should have eight to ten toys to ensure they always have something interesting. Providing a variety of toys helps you figure out which ones really float your cats' boat—different kitties may have different tastes. Rotate three or four at a time to keep them fresh and new to the pet.
- Cats have extremely acute hearing and scent sense. If they chew a wall or baseboard, consider there may be "critters" running around inside the walls that prompt the behavior. Trap or otherwise remove rodents or insects that drive your pet buggy.
- Some cats damage windowsills or pull down drapes when they see another animal outside trespassing on their territory. Blocking access to the window and view of the interloper often stops the behavior. Keep windows closed and move furniture to block access.

CLAW CONDUCT

Nothing looks more appealing than a fluffy, cuddly kitten—until the claws come out. Clawing is hard-wired into the feline brain, and is a natural instinctive behavior that can't be stopped. Claws are the equivalent of human finger- and toenails, and composed of hard, nonliving protein (cuticle) that grows from the nerve and blood-rich quick. Feline claws arise from the last joint of each toe, and extend and retract courtesy of two small "hinged" bones that rest nearly on top of each other. When relaxed, claws sheath inside a skin fold so the paws look soft and smooth. Flexing the tendon straightens the folded bones and pushes claws forward and down, spreading paws to almost twice the former width.

Clawing feels good, and provides great aerobic exercise to stretch the shoulder and foreleg muscles. Cats don't wear down their claws during walking about and playing the way dogs do. Clawing objects keeps nails healthy by helping to shed the old layer, and expose the sharp new growth. More importantly, scent pads in kitty paws leave invisible smell-cues of ownership. The visible marks also serve as messages to warn away other cats from prime feline real estate. Cats also claw to soothe upset feelings, and they increase clawing during times of stress—placing a scratch post in areas the cat urine sprays can help by relieving angst with scratching instead.

If Sheba can't reach something she really wants, such as a toy the other cat has swiped, she may claw the post as a displacement behavior instead of aggressing toward the other feline. Other times, she'll use clawing to express positive emotions by running to scratch the post when you return for the day, or she knows the food bowl will be filled. A cat introduced into a new home may turn into a clawing maniac until she becomes more comfortable. Cats also use their claws to protect themselves from threats, and they use scratching as a displacement behavior.

Clipping Claws

Felines are great at bluffing and often "pull their punches" by bopping the nosy dog or other cat with claws withheld. But claws endanger eyes and can hurt your lap when cats indulge in kneading behavior. Even before you train your cats to scratch appropriately, you can protect your furniture and other pets with a feline pedicure.

When your cat relaxes on your lap, or snoozes on the sofa, gently pet her and pick up a paw. Squeeze gently between your thumb and fingers to express the sharp nail tips, and snip off the sharp, white hooked end with your own nail clippers or a pair designed for pets. Avoid the pink "quick" at the base of the toe, which contains the blood supply and will bleed if nicked.

No rule says you must trim every claw at one sitting. Clip only as many as Kitty will allow, and stop before she struggles, then offer her a favorite treat or toy. Clip only two or three a night, offering bribes along the way, and all four paws will be done in a week or so.

COMFORT ZONE

A wide range of scratching objects is available, from fancy multi-tiered "trees" and color-coordinated carpet covered feline furniture to homemade objects available from the back yard. Pet products stores, cat shows, grocery stores, and online sites such as www.angelicat.com offer a variety of commercial products. But cats don't care what you spend, and an inexpensive catnip-impregnated cardboard surface, or a cedar log from Uncle Jim's farm may be your cat's dream-come-true.

Despite all best efforts, some hard-case cats are slow or stubborn and have problems following claw rules. Vinyl nail covers called Soft Paws reduce the potential for scratch damage in these cases. The vinyl caps glue over the top of each nail, and come in a variety of fashion colors. They are available from pet supply stores and some veterinary offices. You can learn to apply them yourself.

Declaw Surgery

Declaw surgery amputates the last joint of each toe to remove the claw and the nail bed from which it grows. Declaw surgery has no health benefits to the cat, and serves only as a convenience for owners. Surveys estimate 25 percent of cats in North America are declawed, but the procedure is condemned and even illegal in many other countries. Professional cat fanciers feel so strongly about this, that pedigreed cats are not allowed to appear in cat shows if they have been declawed.

Surgery does eliminate potential claw damage to your belongings, and some declawed cats never have problems from the surgery. But a percentage of declawed cats become biters and/or develop litter box aversions due to painful paws, creating a host of new behavior issues that impact you and your multipet household. Declawing should not be considered routine, and only considered after exhausting all other options. Veterinary surveys estimate that as many as 50 percent of owners that had a cat declawed wouldn't otherwise have kept the cat.

Kittens recover more quickly than adult cats. Without claws for protection, declawed felines should be kept inside for their safety. The most recent (and humane) surgical techniques employ lasers, resulting in less pain and bleeding during recovery. Talk with your veterinarian and other cat owners before deciding to declaw.

Teaching Claw Etiquette

Most cats can be trained to use appropriate scratching objects, so they can keep their claws. When you introduce a young kitten into an adult cat home, the baby learns more quickly by observing the other felines' good behavior and makes the training job easier.

- A single cat thinks she rules every window, door, feeding station and sleeping area, and a single post may not do justice to her territorial needs. When you have more than one cat, several scratch objects are required. Spread them over the entire house to accommodate all the cats' territory and so one feline can't "guard" and own all the objects.

- Clawing marks territory so scratch objects must be located correctly for the cat to use them. Kitty wants the world to see his scratch-graffiti and won't use objects hidden in back rooms so place posts in high traffic areas or near important cat territory: lookouts, food stations, and your bedroom (if you share a pillow).

- To accommodate the cats' exercise and stretching needs, the scratch object must be long or tall enough to accommodate their full stretch, and stable enough to withstand an all-out assault. Kittens outgrow small posts and need an upgrade once they're mature. If the post tips over onto the cat, you'll have an awful time convincing Sheba to try again.

- The scratch surface, size and the shape of the post are also important. Cats have individual surface preferences such as wood, sisal or carpet, as well as posture preferences. Some like to stretch out on tummies to scratch horizontal surfaces, while others like vertical scratching, so observe your cats to figure out what they like or offer several kinds for them to choose.

- Spike new scratch objects with catnip to promote feline allegiance. Play-oriented cats can be lured to try out the post by dragging a feather or other toy across the surface, so they sink in claws. Don't be afraid to demonstrate claw technique to Kitty, either. Cats learn by mimicking behavior, so the demonstration by you (or another feline) can help because it also marks the post with your scent, making it an even more attractive object for the cats to claim as their own.

- Cats that have already clawed furniture or carpet return to the scene of the crime to refresh the marks/scent, unless they have better options. Place the new "legal" scratch object directly in front of the damaged sofa or on top of the clawed carpet. Once the cat begins to use the legal object, you can slowly move it (a foot at a time) to a more convenient location that's still within the cat's territorial ideal.

- Physical punishment or even a loud scolding cause fear and increased anxiety for the cat. Instead, use interruption to stop the behavior. Cats often scratch without conscious thought sort of like you tapping your fingers. Other cats test you, and only behave when you enforce the rules. Slap a newspaper against your thigh, clap hands, or shake an empty soda can full of pennies to stop Sheba in mid-claw. A long-distance squirt gun aimed at a furry tail can startle some cats out of the behavior; however, some cats like to be sprayed. Once kitty stops, direct claws to the legal target with the feather toy, and praise when she does the right thing.

- Interruptions are most effective if you stay silent, with little to no movement while giving the interruption. Doing so out of sight is even more effective but hard to do. A remote control 'booby trap' can be helpful. Try hooking up an alarm, hair dryer, Water Pik or tape recording into a remote switch and place in the area where the cat misbehaves. Watch for illegal activity and trigger the interruption when the cat enters the area.

- Make illegal targets unattractive to the cats, so that they'll leave them alone even when you're not around. There are several good claw-deterrents available, but not all work for every cat, so experiment until one works for you. One of the most effective for on upholstery is a double-sided tape product called Sticky Paws (www.stickypaws.com). Cats dislike touching surfaces that stick to paw fur, and this often keeps claws at bay.

- An innovative new training product called the Ssscat™ aerosol, available at www.premier.com, gives off a HISSS of air that trains cats to scat when a motion detector triggered by their presence sets it off. You don't have to be there for it to work.

- A product called Feliway duplicates the cheek scent that cats produce to rub against furniture, your ankles, the dog, or other objects. The pheromone reduces environmental stress that prompts excessive clawing, and since cats don't want to scratch on top of a cheek-marked area, you can use Feliway to prevent illegal scratching. For best results, spray the forbidden area once a day, while providing a "legal" target. You can find Feliway at most pet products stores.

- Strong scents such as citrus deodorants, Vicks or No Scratch from pet stores repel many cats. Apply directly to forbidden objects or on fabric draped over the problem area.
- Cinnamon peppered on dark upholstery, or baby powder on light fabric, prompts a poof of scented dust into the cat's face when she assaults with feline claws. Both the dust and the scent help remind cats of their manners even when you aren't around to supervise.
- Claws hitting bubble-wrap taped to an illegal target POP! and interrupt kitty scratching. Remember, booby-traps aren't permanent, but offer interim teaching aids to transition Sheba to a legal target. Once she uses the right scratching object, you can remove the bubble wrap or other decorator's eyesores.

More Paw Behavior: Kneading

Cats use their sensitive paws to test objects for safety. Soft tentative taps measure temperature, texture and density and can be aimed at toys, other cats or humans. Paw thumps may be used to discipline or to invite play.

A kitten's rhythmic paw-pushing with front paws, termed kneading behavior, stimulates the release of a mother cat's milk. It looks similar to how bread dough is made. The behavior doesn't stop when nursing goes away, though. Even adult cats knead against soft objects like your thigh or a pillow when they seem to feel particularly happy and satisfied.

We suspect the emotions hearken back to feel-good moments of nursing during kittenhood. So adult cats who knead an owner's lap may actually be declaring their love for a surrogate human "mom."

Rear Foot Treading

Cats may rear foot tread during play. It looks sort of like a "rev your engines" preparation for a game of cat-tag. The hunter typically crouches in a stalking pose and rear-foot treads just before racing to pounce on the mouse.

Intact male cats also rear-paw tread after mounting a female cat during breeding. Some cats also use rear paw scraping after urine spraying or leaving a deposit in the litter box. Kicking up some dirt not only leaves scent marks from paw pads, it may also leave visual cues.

COUNTERTOP CRUISING

Cats naturally adore high places because they're safe lookouts and make a literal statement about the cat's place in the feline hierarchy. However, countertop cruising can be both a safety and a hygiene issue for owners and the cats. Nobody enjoys having a pet "graze" from the dinner table or skillet, and walking across a hot stovetop may cause serious burns.

Dealing with height-loving felines frustrates owners. Even when Kitty understands that a particular location (the mantel) is forbidden, she may avoid the place when you're present, but plant her furry tail on high as soon as you leave the room. When you return and she sees you, she'll leap off even before you yell at her. A couple of things are going on. The cat that claims the highest position is the "top cat" in the scheme of feline hierarchy. Cats want to be able to see long distances, and be out of reach of potential threats.

Second, cats practice a time-share mentality, and schedule lounging time to avoid competition, so when the "top cat" is not there to use the preferred perch, the cat feels within her rights to claim it. After all, YOU weren't using it! Then when you catch her in the forbidden zone, she acknowledges you as the top cat and gets off in deference to your social status.

Multiple cats means you'll constantly chase cats off second story space, because as soon as one vacates the real estate, another waits to take her place. When cats must share space with dogs, they'll be even more inclined to take the "high road" and avoid the ground floor territory claimed by any canines. That can be a safety issue as well as a social statement for the cat. You will not win all these battles, but you can modify some of these irksome behaviors, and encourage cats to stay off forbidden places with training techniques.

- When you are there, use an interruption, such as a loud "OFF!" or clapped hands to get cats down. A long-distance squirt gun aimed at the backside may persuade some cats.
- When you aren't around, the cat will still use the perch unless you make it unattractive. Cover stovetops with aluminum foil. Many cats dislike walking on this surface.
- Apply Sticky Paws (double-sided tape) to make other surfaces uncomfortable. Put the Sticky Paws on placemats set around on forbidden surfaces, so you can easily position them but remove

them when needed. You can also use clear plastic floor mats placed spike-side up on tabletops so cats will avoid the area.

- Offer your cats legal outlets that are higher and more attractive than the forbidden zones, so they naturally choose the legal perches and leave your mantel alone. Cat trees are a big hit. Fancy ones are available from pet products stores, or you can make inexpensive fun feline furniture out of a ladder. Tie toys and ribbons onto the rungs, place a fluffy cat bed on the paint rack, glue rope around and around a step for a scratch surface, and you have an innovative cat gymnasium.

- Choose your battles and perhaps allow cats to lounge on the television as long as they leave the kitchen island alone. Place a cat bed on a "legal" countertop or bookshelf to invite the cats' presence and they'll be less likely to trespass where not welcome.

COMFORT ZONE

An innovative new training product called the SSSCAT combines aerosol and a motion detector to get cats to move their furry tail OFF of forbidden real estate. When the cat's presence sets off the motion detector, it triggers a loud HISS of air to startle the cat away from the area. You don't have to be present for it to work.

DOOR DASHING

Cats seem to assume that doors are a challenge, sort of a game of "chicken" to race to the other side before it catches their tail. Door dashing not only can prove to be a tripping hazard for owners, cats that get outside may become lost and never return.

Cat escape artists can be extra difficult when you have more than one feline determined to door dash. While cats get very good at avoiding forbidden areas when you are nearby, the appearance of a visitor or

salesperson at the door can be invitation to zoom out before you've realized
what happened. Stop door dashers with these tips.

- **Make Doors Unattractive.** Associate the danger areas with a noise
  or experience that encourages the cat to keep her distance. An
  interruption such as a loud "SSST!" or clapped hands may be
  enough. Squirt guns aimed at furry tails often are recommended and
  cats do learn to back off when they see owners pick up the plant
  mister. But many cats enjoy games of water tag, or the spray doesn't
  matter to them, so it's not a failsafe or reliable technique. The
  SSSCAT is a cat-repellent device that sprays a hiss of air to startle
  the pet that triggers the built-in motion detector-you don't have to
  be present for it to work.
- **Create Off-Putting Surfaces.** Many cats dislike the feeling of
  walking on aluminum foil, so place a couple of sheets over the
  walkway. Another option is to apply Sticky Paws (double-sided
  tape) to make the surface uncomfortable. Put the Sticky Paws on
  placemats positioned on the forbidden area, so it's easily removed.
  You can also use clear plastic floor mats placed spike-side up so the
  cat will avoid the area.
- **Make It Stink.** You may also use smell deterrents to keep the cat
  away from forbidden doorway zones. Cats dislike citrus smells, so
  orange or lemon scents sprayed at the bottom of the door may help.
  Menthol also makes some cats run (but others like the smell). Try
  smearing Vicks on the door jamb to see if that will give your cats
  pause.
- **Offer Something Better.** Offer cats legal outlets that are more
  attractive than the forbidden zones, and they'll naturally choose to
  lounge there and abandon the doorway dash. Position a cat tree or
  kitty bed on a table top right in front of a window some distance
  away from the forbidden door. Make this the most wonderful cat
  lounge spot ever: hide catnip or food treats in the bed, for example.
- **Distract With Goodies.** Before you must leave through the
  doorway, offer your cats the best-treat-in-the-world, but only if
  she's on this cat tree/bed (a safe distance from the door). While
  they enjoy the munchies, make a safe getaway.
- **Practice Your Escape.** Get friends to help you set up practice
  comings and goings. Associate the ringing doorbell with treats in

the cat tree/bed. That helps your cats learn that door dashes earn nothing while sitting in place garner treats.

DOWN TO EARTH

Cats enjoy recreational digging in terms of scooping out and covering up a toilet spot. They particularly relish fine, soft textures, which means the soil in the indoor potted palm or freshly planted garden may receive unwanted attention. They'll also dig in these areas if their litter box situation doesn't please them. Understanding why cats dig can help you figure out ways to stem the excavation.

- Cats seek alternate places to "go" when their own facilities are dirty, so keep litter boxes clean. Some cats won't want to share a bathroom, so provide one litter box for each cat, plus one. Refer to the chapter on Toilet Techniques for more litter box advice.
- Sticky Paws for Plants works well to keep indoor plants safe from indoor pets. You can also turn plastic carpet runners nub-side up and set the potted plant in the middle, so the cats avoid walking on the nubs to reach the soil.
- Keep your own cats inside to prevent them using your garden as a bathroom.
- Dissuade strays by scattering orange or lemon rinds in the flower beds (they hate the smell of citrus), or planting rue—a natural cat repellent used by the ancient Egyptians. Refer to the section on shooing away stray cats for more tips.

DROOLING CATS

Why do some cats drool when petted? A bubble-blowing saliva-spewing kitty can be quite off-putting to owners seeking to show affection.

Sometimes drooling points to dental issues or sore mouths. While the sight of something tasty can get dogs soaking wet with slobber, the same thing rarely seems to happen with cats. When a cat feels stressed, excessive grooming may be a way she helps calm herself and increases salivation.

But some cats salivate when petted. The more they get petted, the greater the drippy flow. The mechanism to turn on the water works has to do with the same pleasure triggers that prompt petted cats to knead/tread in satisfaction.

Cats' impulse to knead hearkens back to the sensation they felt when nursing, and eating would trigger salivation. So it's not a huge jump to attribute salivating and drooling to these same pleasurable sensations. Drooling when petted is one more way cats show us love.

ELEVATOR BUTT

The technical term is lordosis, although pet owners may describe the position as "elevator butt." This common cat pose looks like the canine play-bow in which the front paws and tummy touch the ground while the other end stands tall.

Lordosis posture serves as the intact female cat's romantic invitation to males as a mating display. Some cats also use this position when urine marking, to spray their pungent scent higher or with better aim.

Neutered cats also practice the elevator butt pose around humans. The display places the cat in a vulnerable position, often with the tail held high in the universal feline friendly gesture. Cats also may do this to invite petting or scratching that hard-to-reach spot right at the base of the tail.

Elevator butt aimed at humans is a declaration of friendship, and an invitation to come closer and interact. By scratching or petting your cat in response, you reinforce the behavior so the cat will repeat the gesture. Petting also tells the cat you accept the offer of friendship.

GRASS EATING

Cats are obligate carnivores, which mean they require meat to survive. They do not rely on vegetables, fruit or grain in the diet, no matter what might be on the pet food ingredient list. But pet cats can't read and seem intent on surprising us. Many cats relish grazing on grass, flowers or other vegetation.

In the wild, cats eat the entire mouse. Partially digested plant or grain material in a victim's tummy offers nutrients that cats readily use.

Eating grass may also provide trace elements of vitamins that cats instinctively seek. It may also help provide fiber to move out hairballs or act as an emetic to clean kitty out from the other direction.

It's likely that cats simply enjoy the flavor. Wheat grass often is a big hit, and fresh catnip is a lovely feline treat particularly useful as a training tool.

HUNTING GIFTS

Cats have been domesticated for centuries but the wild child remains just beneath the fur. Many cats become expert hunters adept at capturing critters, be they a feather toy on the end of a string, a cricket at the door, or even a mouse or lizard. Sheba doesn't have to be hungry to hunt, either. Well-fed cats hunt better, because they have the energy to burn. The behavior is hardwired in the cat brain so that the scurrying motion and ultrasonic squeak simply triggers a knee-jerk (paw-jerk?) reaction to pounce.

So what do these well-fed cats do once they've captured that ferocious moth, or decapitated the vole? If they love you, some cats share the bounty. Such "gifts" may be displayed on the back step, in their food bowl, or even on your pillow.

The cat believes she's offering you the ultimate compliment when she presents the result of her prowess for your inspection. Some behaviorists believe these cats look on their humans as inept hunters unable to bring home the bacon (or butterfly) without feline assistance. After all, she's never seen YOU get down on all fours and pounce on your evening meal! These cats may even bring home live prey, and turn it loose in the house, much as they would do to train a kitten the ABCs of hunting.

Other experts theorize the cat simply brings her trophy to her nest—the house—with plans to play with, enjoy, and munch later. How frustrated our kitties must be to have their plans thwarted by dense, unappreciative humans.

Wearing a bell on the collar may help give the cat's prey an early warning, and prevent or reduce the number of nasty gifts you receive. However, truly proficient cat hunters learn to move without ever ringing that bell. A better way to thwart the behavior is to simply keep the cat inside, and provide your indoor tiger with alternative toys.

Of course, some houses are more critter-proof than others. Critters crawl under doorways, or enter through attic spaces and (maybe?) deserve what they get from the resident feline. So, what's a sensitive, caring owner to do when presented with these nasty gifts?

Smile, praise the cat, let him or her preen with pride when you extol exceptional hunting prowess. Then (when kitty isn't looking) carefully dispose of the trophy and perhaps replace it with a more wholesome treat.

ROLLING CATS

A common cat behavior incorporates head-rubbing behavior with rolling about on the ground. Vocalizations may be included. Cats roll for several reasons.

Female cats roll in this manner immediately after mating. Similar rolling behavior occurs in cats during catnip intoxication, which is one reason the herb used to be thought to be a feline aphrodisiac. But cats roll at other times, too, and what does it mean when in the presence of humans?

Dogs roll onto their back as a sign of deference or submission. But a cat on her back can be a defensive pose since it places all four clawed paws at the ready. In a defensive situation, though, the cat tends to remain still and vocalizations are defensive in nature (hisses, growls, spits).

The cat that throws herself at the feet of the owner may accompany the behavior with meows. This pose along with meows, rolling and rubbing the floor asks for attention and is a solicitation display. Rolling also spreads self-scent when Kitty rubs her head and cheeks on the floor, as well as providing a self-massage.

Cats love routine, so once a pattern is established, the rolling also becomes a comforting kitty ritual. Giving her attention in response to the rolling rewards the behavior—positive reinforcement that "pays" her for rolling. The cat that garners positive attention with rolling will repeat the behavior for more attention.

TELEPHONE TROUBLES

When the phone rings, many cats come running. A few become aggressive and have been known to bite through the phone cord. But the majority just turns into pestering problems. Why do cats have a love-hate relationship with the phone? Are cats jealous of you chatting with your BFF?

While acute sense of hearing might make it possible for cats to recognize a particular voice on the other end of the line, cats more likely don't understand the notion of such long distance communication. It's more likely that the ringtone simply prompts interest and the cat associates that sound with a benefit that rewards the pestering behavior.

Cats learn that using the phone typically happens in a specific place. Maybe that means you're seated at a desk or pacing in the family room. My own cat knows that phone calls generally nail me in place for the duration.

Further, when you speak on the phone the cat only sees you present. Since our pets quickly learn that humans talk to communicate, and nobody else is there, cats must think we're talking to them. Therefore, when owners pick up the phone, cats respond with attention-seeking behaviors such as meows, head rubs and rolling.

When owners respond to the cat's solicitations, they've reinforced the behavior. That increases the likelihood that the next phone call will bring on even more meows and "pet me" demands.

TOILET PESTS

Cats often eagerly follow owners into the bathroom. If you close the door in the cat's face she may pester with paw-reaches under the door. What's going on?

Human bathrooms tend to be one of the coolest places in the home, because of the tile, small space, and typically fewer windows. While many cats enjoy warmth, others prefer cool lounging spots like the tile surrounding the tub.

Cats also develop routines and stick to them, including chaining behaviors that link one action to another in a particular routine. In other words, cats become used to the sequence of actions, and anticipate/expect them to be repeated day in and day out. It only takes one or two repetitions for cats to learn that every morning when you wake up, you head to the bathroom to brush your teeth—so they meet you there.

Besides, the bathrooms generally offer very convenient cat perches. Sitting on the sink surround or vanity places a cat at human face-height when the owner is (ahem) enthroned. That's ideal cat position for controlling the interaction. Owners will be in position for a specific amount of time, and won't move away. The cat can approach (or stay out of reach) as she prefers with this captive audience.

Bathroom visits offer predictable behavior, and a specific location(s) the cat can anticipate. Each time the owner enters that room the cat can know in advance what sorts of behaviors to expect. There also can be a number of rewards to be found, such as lapping from the faucet. A closed door offers paw-pat-tag underneath the barrier, and may challenge cats to perfect their door dashing technique.

When you talk to or pet your bathroom buddy, turn on the faucet, or bring in a brush for grooming, you've rewarded the behavior. Cats may even decide that the under-the-door paw-pats that start as a game actually controls the movement of the door. After all, the longer those paw-pats continue, the better becomes the chance that you will eventually open the door.

APPENDICES

EXPERT SOURCES

Bonnie Beaver, MS, DVM, is a behaviorist and chief of medicine in the Department of Small Animal Medicine and Surgery at the College of Veterinary Medicine at Texas A & M University

Sharon L. Crowell-Davis, DVM is a veterinarian and a behaviorist at the College of Veterinary Medicine at the University of Georgia

Ian Dunbar, Ph.D., MRCVS, is a veterinarian and animal behaviorist, author of many dog training books, and a founder of the Association of Pet Dog Trainers.

Bruce D. Elsey, DVM is a veterinarian, owner of a cats-only practice, and creator of Cat Attract cat litter

Gary Lansberg, BSc, DVM, Diplomate ACVB, is a veterinary behaviorist at the Doncaster Animal Clinic in Thornhill, Ontario

Marie-Laure Loubiere, DVM is a veterinarian involved in pheromone research and marketing with CEVA Santé Animal S.A., in France.

Andrew U. Luescher, DVM, PhD., Diplomate ACVB is an Associate Professor of Animal Behavior at Purdue University

Karen Overall, DVM, Diplomate ACVB, ABS, is a Research Associate at the Center for Neurobiology and Behavior, Psychiatry Department at Penn Med, PA

Patricia McConnell, Ph.D., is a certified Applied Animal Behaviorist and an adjunct assistant professor of zoology at the University of Wisconsin-Madison

Daniel Mills, BVSc, PhD is a researcher into pheromone applications and Principle lecturer in behavioral studies and animal welfare at the University of Lincoln in the United Kingdom

Patrick Pageat, DVM, PhD, is a Behaviorist Diplomate of the French National Veterinary Schools, and Research and Development Director of Pherosynthese s.n.c.

Patricia Pryor, DVM, Diplomate ACVB is an assistant professor in the Veterinary Behavior Services at Washington State University

Kersti Seskel, BVSc, MRCVS, FACUSc, MACVSc (Animal Behavior), is a veterinarian and behaviorist practicing at Seaforth Veterinary Hospital in Sydney, Australia

ANIMAL BEHAVIOR SOURCES

There are several behavior organizations with professionals available who specialize in pet training and/or behavior problems. Behaviors such as aggression can be difficult to unlearn and require professional help to teach cats how to react in new, more positive ways.

THE AMERICAN COLLEGE OF VETERINARY BEHAVIORISTS

Veterinarians with a special interest and additional study in the field of animal behavior. As veterinarians, they are also able to diagnose concurrent health conditions and prescribe drug therapies that may be helpful. http://www.veterinarybehaviorists.org

THE ANIMAL BEHAVIOR SOCIETY

Certifies qualified individuals as Applied or Associate Applied Animal Behaviorists http://animalbehaviorsociety.org

THE INTERNATIONAL ASSOCIATION OF ANIMAL BEHAVIOR CONSULTANTS, INC.

A professional organization that accredits and qualifies members as Certified Animal Behavior Consultants (CABC), and addresses behavior issues of cats, dogs, and other companion animals. http://www.iaabc.org

FURTHER READING
Books by Amy Shojai

CAT FACTS: THE PET PARENT'S A-TO-Z HOME CARE ENCYCLOPEDIA

COMPETABILITY: SOLVING BEHAVIOR PROBLEMS IN YOUR CAT/DOG HOUSEHOLD

COMPLETE CARE FOR YOUR AGING CAT

COMPLETE KITTEN CARE

MY CAT HATES MY VET! FOILING FEAR BEFORE, DURING & AFTER VET VISITS

NEW CHOICES IN NATURAL HEALING FOR DOGS & CATS

THE FIRST AID COMPANION FOR DOGS & CATS

AFTERWORD

Many years ago, more than I care to admit, I became an accidental pet writer.

I grew up rescuing orphan bunnies and baby birds fallen from nests, turning turtles and snakes into pets, and luring squirrels and raccoons to eat from my hand. I loved feeding Grandma's chickens, horseback riding, and milking the cows (or trying to).

But my deepest affection was for dogs and cats.

It seemed fated when I found a job as a veterinary technician and met countless caring owners. But many felt frustrated by their relationships, and all too often, heartbreak resulted. I never set out to be a writer, and my career as a pet journalist would never have happened without the countless veterinarians, behaviorists, trainers, researchers, and pet lovers who put up with my endless questions. Thank you!

If you're reading this, you belong to the "pet generation," part of the 60+ percent of U.S. households that keep cats and dogs. The more time we spend with our cats and dogs, the stronger our bond becomes. The medical profession has legitimized these attachments through multiple research studies that prove the positive impact pets have on human health. So, while in the past we may not have admitted these affections, today our love affair with pets has become a very public one. Deep affection toward and a new awareness of our enhanced relationship with pets—and the way cats and dogs relate to each other—drives today's owner to seek the most current, highest quality behavior care to preserve this loving bond.

This dedication toward pets isn't surprising. Economic conditions that prompt young professionals to delay marriage and/or children can result in them lavishing affection and attention on their pets. But emotional attachment to pets continues when owners marry and start families. Pet love only begins there—older people relish the interaction and unconditional love offered by dogs and cats.

This book offers prescriptive solutions for the owners of multiple pets, to help you better understand how cats think, relate to each other, and can best be taught to follow your rules and get along. It provides quick answers to common everyday concerns, helps improve pet behavior, and provides information that allows pets to live longer and healthier lives. I've presented information in an easy-to-use format with step-by-step tips to help readers build their very own peaceable kingdom.

I'm confident "ComPETability" will help you and your multi-pet family. Pets have certainly changed my life for the better, and I hope my writing will make a positive difference in the lives of cats, dogs, and those who love them.

INDEX

T

U

V

W

Y

Z

Amy Shojai, CABC is a certified animal behavior consultant and a nationally known authority on pet care. She is the award-winning author of 30 cat and dog books and thousands of articles and columns. She hosted a weekly half-hour Pet Peeves radio show, and has written behavior columns at dozens of print and online venues including cats.About.com, PetSafe.com, Purina's CatChow.com and her PETiQuette newspaper column. Amy addresses a wide range of fun-to-serious issues in her work, covering training, behavior, health care, and medical topics.

Amy is a founder and president emeritus of the Cat Writers Association, Inc., a member of the Dog Writers' Association of America, past president of Oklahoma Writers Federation, Inc., and an active member of International Thriller Writers. She frequently speaks to groups on a variety of pet-centric issues, lectures at writing conferences, and regularly appears on national radio and television including Animal Planet CATS 101.

She and her husband live with the Siamese "wannabe" Seren, Karma-Kat, and Magic the German shepherd, and 700+ roses at their north Texas "spread." Amy can be reached at her website at www.shojai.com where you can subscribe to her PETS PEEVES Newsletter and follow her Bling, Bitches & Blood Blog.

Please consider recommending COMPETABLITY to your rescue organizations and cat-loving friends. Help other kitty lovers benefit from the information in this book by writing a review.

Made in the USA
Middletown, DE
08 April 2018